JEAN DUBUFFET: A Retrospective

JEAN DUBUFFET

A Retrospective

This project is supported by a grant from the

National Endowment for the Arts in

Washington, D. C., a Federal Agency,

and a grant from the Association

française d'Action artistique

Published by The Solomon R. Guggenheim Foundation, New York, 1973

Library of Congress Card Catalogue Number: 73-77081

© The Solomon R. Guggenheim Foundation, 1973

Printed in the United States

ERRATA

p. 37
Title should read *Allocution faite à l'occasion de l'inauguration du groupe de quatre arbres*

p. 69
No. 30 should read *Edith Boissonnas démon thibétain*

p. 83
No. 44 should read *Le Métafizyx*

p. 106
No. 67 should read *Le Dépenaillé*

p. 278
No. 284 should read *Paysage contrapontique*

p. 295
No. 295 b should read *Masque de théâtre XIV (Le Postulant)*

p. 300
1957, stays at Le Touquet began in 1962
1968, title of exhibition at Musée des Arts Décoratifs should read *Edifices*

p. 303
Title for Fascicule XXIV should read *Tour aux figures, amoncellements, Cabinet logologique* (Tower with figures, accumulations, Logological cabinet)

Nos. 26, 69, 294 not in exhibition

Lenders List

Julian J. Aberbach
Mr. and Mrs. Walter Bareiss
Dr. and Mrs. Irwin R. Berman
J. M. de Broglie, Paris
Mr. and Mrs. Gordon Bunshaft, New York
Norman B. Champ, Jr.
Alphonse Chave
Mr. and Mrs. Ralph F. Colin, New York
Hubert and F. Teri Damisch, Paris
Mr. and Mrs. Charles M. Diker
Edward F. Dragon, East Hampton, New York
Gerard Louis-Dreyfus, New York
Jean Dubuffet
Lucien Durand, Paris
Robert Elkon, New York
Mr. and Mrs. Richard L. Feigen, Bedford, New York
Mr. and Mrs. Martin A. Fisher, New York
Arnold and Milly Glimcher, New York
Mrs. Eva Glimcher, Columbus, Ohio
Paul Glimcher, New York
Roger Goldet, Neuilly, France
Miss Elizabeth Hahn, New York
Stephen Hahn, New York
Mr. and Mrs. Morton L. Janklow, New York
Edwin Janss, Jr., Thousand Oaks, California
Dr. and Mrs. Marvin E. Klein
Mr. and Mrs. Arthur J. Kobacker, Steubenville, Ohio
Walter Lees, Paris
Mrs. Warner Leroy, New York
Mrs. M. Victor Leventritt
Mr. and Mrs. Robert E. Linton
Max Loreau, Belgium
André Malraux
Dr. and Mrs. Abraham Melamed
Franz Meyer, Basel
Robert and Jane Meyerhoff
Mr. and Mrs. N. Richard Miller
Mr. and Mrs. Myron A. Minskoff
Fred Mueller
Dr. Arthur J. Neumann, New York
Mr. and Mrs. Morton Neumann

Acknowledgements

Thomas M. Messer, Director
The Solomon R.
Guggenheim Museum

A major retrospective exhibition of Jean Dubuffet's work had been sought by the Guggenheim Museum for a long time. It was first spoken of when I proposed it to the artist during his visit to the Guggenheim in October 1966, on the occasion of the first American museum survey of his *Hourloupe* series. Upon Dubuffet's acceptance, the Centre National d'Art Contemporain in Paris announced its eagerness to present Dubuffet's work, also in extensive scope, at the Grand Palais, to fall within a series of grand homages accorded to French masters of the twentieth century. Discussions, therefore, were initiated with Blaise Gautier, the Centre National d'Art Contemporain's director, which resulted in an agreement to unite our respective efforts in a common cause and to present essentially the same exhibition in New York and in Paris. Fruitful and mutually gratifying cooperation between the two museum organizations ensued in the intervening years.

A retrospective of such magnitude cannot be attempted without the agreement of key lenders to support the exhibition project. The artist himself and major collectors of his work were initially committed and eventually joined by many others, to whom both organizing institutions are deeply and sincerely grateful. The sacrifices made by individuals willing to deprive themselves for an extended period of time of cherished objects, and the readiness of many museums to entrust their possessions to our care may be justified only by one consideration: to show a meaningful sequence selected from the life-work of a great contemporary artist in two metropolitan centers of art. This catalogue, also produced in cooperation with our Parisian colleagues, reflects such a choice by listing a total of 296 works, all destined to fill the spaces of the Guggenheim and (with some inevitable substitutions) those of the Grand Palais.

The large and responsible task of selection and the organization of the catalogue has been entrusted to Margit Rowell who, throughout the project, acted as the exhibition's curator. In the course of her search, no effort was spared to present Dubuffet's creative evolution through a carefully considered chronological sequence and to render it meaningful through the finest examples obtainable.

The usual framework of such a project (with its double dimension of exhibition and catalogue) has, in this case, been extended through the addition of a performance, also rooted in Jean Dubuffet's art. The event, entitled *Coucou Bazar,* is, in fact, subject to a double reading: as kinetic extension of the show itself, or as a performing-arts parallel of it. It was staged by Brooke Lappin and his colleagues in close cooperation with, indeed upon instruction by, Jean Dubuffet himself.

Organization and selection of this retrospective, publication of the catalogue and production of *Coucou Bazar,* the financing of the undertaking, and the final presentation of all parts, has proven to be a task as taxing as it has been rewarding for those involved in it. Many individuals, within and outside of this museum made valuable contributions. They are too numerous to be thanked individually and will, I trust, accept the collective thanks offered them most sincerely herewith. Even in a summary acknowledgement, however, we cannot avoid naming the loyal members of Dubuffet's Secrétariat, Mrs. Armande de Trentinian and Miss Pascale Flavigny for their unflagging efforts on our behalf. We are also grateful to Pierre de Montbas for his assistance on this project, as well as to Arnold Glimcher of the Pace Gallery for his generous and enthusiastic cooperation.

Last, our joint and deep gratitude goes to Jean Dubuffet who has honored our initiative with his interest and his sympathy and who, in behalf of all of us, has not hesitated to assume burdens that went far beyond any reasonable expectation.

Introduction

Thomas M. Messer

Jean Dubuffet's sharp profile began to delineate itself in the middle of the nineteen-forties against the pale background of the postwar School of Paris. His final emergence, after a number of false starts, was timely, and his rude disturbance of efforts to continue the great modern traditions in diluted form evoked anguished outcries from the world of institutionalized culture. It was then that Dubuffet's iconoclastic identity was established through the provocative projection of his brute images, his artless techniques and his relentless anticultural stance. Thirty years later, Dubuffet remains a harsh opponent of cultural pretension and a fervent partisan of original, indigenous expression. During these three decades, however, the artist has undertaken an investigation of formal possibilities which, in scope and thoroughness, is probably without equal in our time. The Dubuffet of the seventies, therefore, cannot be seen solely through preconceptions deriving from his work of the forties. Even then, the earthy, passionate and creatively destructive image, which he projected so powerfully, was balanced by a less visible but nonetheless insistent alter ego that strove, on its own terms, for order and authority. Through encompassing both the Dionysian and the Apollonian, Dubuffet exemplifies the paradox without which his art eludes us. This paradox is based upon awareness of the fundamental cohesion between polarities and a capacity to reach out for the grand embrace that brings contraries into a tense, oscillating harmony.

Dubuffet had already come to clear conclusions about the nature of art in his gestative period. It was obvious to him that art differed from what it was often thought to be, and that neither the mimetic figurations demanded by an untaught public nor the abstract essences dear to the culturally affected were worth his time or his effort. Art, in contrast, was the place where ultimate issues hung in the balance. To reach and rejoin that place, Dubuffet opted for the direct and potent language of materials. He knew that their mysterious power to become carriers of thought was based upon their participation in the shaping and forming processes and, therefore, invited them into a threefold partnership with himself and his subject matter. Materials (*matière*) assumed a key position during the forties and fifties, when the artist's efforts were bent upon the destruction of the false gods of culture.

Dubuffet's obsessive preoccupation with *matière* and his eventual return to form is the central theme of Max Loreau's recent book *Jean Dubuffet: Délits, déportements, lieux de haut jeu.* Dubuffet's chronicler sees the years of intensive *matière* exploration not only in terms of the artist's primary reliance upon his means, but as an effort to raise *matière* from its classic subservience to a level of equality with form and even of dominance over it. *Matière,* described by Loreau as the despised component of an art-view dominated by non-material thought, must be brought to assert its superior reality-substance in a struggle with the form complement that, by itself, is doomed to a thin and sterile ideated existence. As the argument develops, form is equated with culture (in Dubuffet's pejorative sense) while *matière* becomes the carrier of an anticultural position—the concrete parallel to creation itself. The phases of Dubuffet's evolution, after the abandonment of the still pictorial *Marionnettes,* first set the stage for a *matière*/form confrontation and then carried it through to its ultimate consequence. The various departures are well known and reappear here as the subject of the current retrospective which presents Dubuffet's work in unprecedented fullness. His portraits, the grotesque landscapes, the fierce images of the *Corps de dames,* various modes of assemblage, his concern with texture and many other phases may be read, even though not deliberately intended, as assaults of the *matière* component against form; and by extension, as the advance of creation against culture. The final chapter in the elevation of *matière* to the detriment of form, is devoted to the *matériologies,* "a veritable desert of form destruction," a phase seemingly foreclosing continuation by its finality. In the context proposed by Loreau, the *Hourloupe* redresses the balance and provides a formula for continuity by clothing form in a self-mocking figuration, and by locking it in an unbreakable embrace with the opposing *matière* ingredient. The latter, in turn, is reduced to its original, clandestine role. Paradoxically, this precarious artifice has attained great solidity. For the artist, it secured a measure of detachment as he delegated to the rearranged components the self-perpetuating life of the work of art.

The *Hourloupe* appears first as a subconscious ball-point doodle, translates itself into painting, reliefs, sculpture, architectural environments and, eventually, into a still nameless theatrical idiom. It is based on a contrived system of planes and stripes carried out in red and blue on black or white and, in its three-dimensional realization, through materials (styrofoam) that suggest an ephemeral, labile unreality. The new, conditional accommodation with form, as Loreau points out, is achieved through *false* means that are charged with the attainment of *virtual* ends.

The importance of the proposed theses lies in the conception of Dubuffet's evolution in terms of a continuous entity; it implicitly rejects a contemplation of the artist's work in two separate parts. A unified view of Dubuffet's work may also be attained by accepting the *Hourloupe* style as a reenactment of earlier material phases. Dubuffet's tendency to elaborate, through *Hourloupe* devices, images conceived and expressed earlier, suggests that it is the point of reference more than the content in his art that had undergone a basic transformation. In Dubuffet, as in Goethe's *Faust,* part I is world exploration—a search for knowledge about man on a profound level of existence. Parts II, in Faust as well as in Dubuffet, transfer this search from the familiar world-frame to an unknown, virtual plane where analogous subject matter relives a now transcended existence. In these spheres, the passionate and earthy, the material dimension of the human condition, are supplanted by a parallel of wider scope and of greater symbolic reach. The *Hourloupe,* if only by implication, continues to explore the human predicament; but the context has shifted with the transferral onto an inhuman landscape, far removed from the phenomena of nature which Dubuffet came to know so well and had explored so deeply.

This Retrospective will show that Dubuffet's life-work is of one piece. Diversity, inconsistency, even Dubuffet's propensity for "error," do not reduce but strengthen the total significance of his central contribution. Today Dubuffet stands before us as a force which, despite itself, has entered and determined the mainstream of a reformed cultural outlook.

Jean Dubuffet:
An Art on the Margins
of Culture

Margit Rowell

Over the span of his thirty-year career, Jean Dubuffet has refused to be *récupéré par la culture* or co-opted by the culture which in 1943 he set out to undermine. Although the major museum retrospectives planned this year in New York and Paris imply popular and official approval, evidence of continuing resistance to his activity proves this implication false. It seems more accurate to suggest that since there is no place for cultural phenomena outside of culture, Dubuffet has been integrated by default into cultural history: his name and myth have been generally accepted in a resigned gesture to the inevitable. He remains nonetheless a thorn in twentieth-century culture's side.

By any standards Dubuffet's work is not "beautiful." It defies the term "interesting." The subject matter is mundane. The visual formulation runs counter to the accepted notions—no matter how elusive—of the work of art in our time. Considered negatively by the viewer, these are positive values in the eyes of the artist, who stated as early as 1945:

> *Personally I am not interested in what is exceptional and this extends to all domains. I feed on the banal. The more banal a thing may be, the better it suits me. Luckily I do not consider myself exceptional in any way. In my paintings, I wish to recover the vision of an average and ordinary man, and, it is without using techniques beyond the grasp of an ordinary man ...that I have tried to constitute great celebrations. Celebrations (or feasts) are much more highly prized when, instead of setting themselves apart on foreign soil...they occur in our everyday life. It is then that their virtue (to transform our daily life into a marvellous feast) is effective. I am speaking of celebrations of the mind; please may it be understood: celebrations of humors and deliriums. Art addresses itself to the mind, not to the eyes. Too many people think that art addresses itself to the eyes. That is to make of it poor use.*

> *Similarly, the most simple and common spectacles appeal to me the most.... I am a tourist of a very special kind: what is picturesque disturbs me. It is where the picturesque is absent that I am in a state of constant amazement.*[1]

Dubuffet was born into a bourgeois family of wine merchants in Le Havre in 1901. He attended the Lycée of Le Havre until 1918 when he received his Baccalaureate degree. The following is the artist's account of his background and his reasons for rejecting it:

1. Jean Dubuffet, *Prospectus et tous écrits suivants*, compiled and edited by Hubert Damisch, Editions Gallimard, Paris, 1967, 2 volumes, vol. II, p. 62. All translations from the French are by the author. Hereafter referred to as *Prospectus*.

After the Lycée, I studied painting for six or seven years as well as many other subjects: poetry, literature, avant-garde, arrière-garde, metaphysics, paleography, ethnography, foreign languages, ancient languages; as you can see I was looking for the Way. Well, it didn't work out; I had the impression that I was not adapted to my human condition; I was slipping around; the gears would not lock into place. After all these years of (half-baked) studies, this accumulation of knowledge (which I forgot as I went along) and systems (which I was constantly changing), in the back of my mind I had this feeling of anxiety that all of it was not worth much . . . in the final analysis, I had missed the boat. . . . When I went to the barber shop in Chaville and observed the men talking to each other, when I listened to the local fireman talking to the butcher or the postman, I felt that they seemed very adapted, so much more adapted than myself. Their accents of joy and certainty made me envious and the idea came to me that in their disjointed conversation there was more sap, more of the unexpected, more invention, in a word more flavor. Let's use the word: there was more art—yes, more art and poetry in the words of the barber —in his life—in his head—than in those of the so-called specialist . . . . And those guys were beating me at my own game . . .

In the streetcar, Dubuffet continued to observe the people around him:

I look at the man sitting opposite me. Tranquil, peaceful face. No problems. Delighted to be alive. Happy to have a seat on the streetcar and to have new shoes. The conductor jokes with him. He answers without thinking, in exactly the right tone. Ah, that cannot be imitated, that tone. The woman next to him, tranquil. Nice intelligent and laughing face. Happy to have earrings, her man out of the hospital, he has a raise. Such faces, full of picturesqueness and personality, full of animation and at the same time profundity, complexity, humanism. In the end I couldn't stand it any longer: I lay down my brushes and I went to work in a wine-shop and subsequently became a wine-dealer . . . [2]

The preceding passages acknowledge a peculiar sense of reality which was to serve as the basis for Dubuffet's mature expression. Significantly, he was not born to the commonplace but adopted it from an outsider's point of view. In 1942, when he left the wine business to take up painting full-time, Dubuffet was neither an untrained artist nor a man without artistic culture. He had attended art school from 1916 to 1920. He had studied art history. In the 1920's in Paris he had been friendly with Max Jacob and members of the Surrealist movement. He had visited the major museums in Europe compiling a repertory of visual motifs, their incidence and variations.[3] Dubuffet's closest friends throughout the forties in Paris were the most brilliant and celebrated literary talents of the time. They included Francis Ponge, Jean Paulhan, Henri Michaux, Georges Limbour, Raymond Queneau and others too numerous to cite. He was also friendly with Jean Fautrier, an abstract painter highly esteemed by a small circle of intellectuals. So that by 1942, Dubuffet was far from uncontaminated by culture. On the contrary, culture was his element. Shedding his acquired ideas would not be easy.

The single most important event in orienting Dubuffet's activity was his discovery of the art of the mentally ill. In 1923, Dubuffet was given a book written by Dr. Hans Prinzhorn: *Bildnerei der Geisteskranken,* published in Berlin the preceding year.[4] When it appeared, this book created a sensation through its assertions that art works executed by asylum inmates were worthy of serious aesthetic consideration. Prinzhorn was also one of the first to draw comparisons between these works and the art of children and of primitive cultures.

To Dubuffet, the book was indeed a revelation, and in it one finds the catalysts, if not the sources, for many of his artistic premises. Prinzhorn's theories echo certain German romantic ideas of the nineteenth and early twentieth centuries. When he speaks of man's natural state as opposed to his cultural (denatured) state—man's primal unity with the universe which has been annihilated by the artificial conventions and repressions of so-called civilization—he evokes Nietzsche and Freud. For Prinzhorn, unfettered basic animal and spiritual drives may lead the individual to psychic strength and harmony with the universe, instead of to neurosis, which is the more common case when he is bound within the confines of Western civilization. To Prinzhorn, the art of the mentally ill manifests a universal creative urge, an urge which cultural inhibitions generally stifle.

Dubuffet projected a similar philosophy in his *Anticultural Positions* speech of 1951. In six points, he expressed his rejection of certain premises of occidental culture and his preference for the spiritual attitudes of primitive peoples:

1. Western man believes that he is very different from other elements of nature such as the wind, trees and rivers. Conversely, primitive man believes that he is of similar substance, that there exists a real continuity between man and nature, and that man is not a superior being but merely one being among many.

3. Dubuffet intended to write a treatise on the development of artists' motifs throughout history. The treatise was not written, but the experience provided him with an invaluable repertory of "cultural" motifs to be avoided when, years later, he adopted his anticultural position.

4. Prinzhorn's book has just been reprinted in English as *Artistry of the Mentally Ill,* Springer-Verlag, New York-Heidelberg-Berlin, 1972.

2. Western man believes that the world exists in the shape that he thinks it, based on reason and logic. Primitive man, on the contrary, rejects logic and respects the states of delirium and madness. Dubuffet confesses to "a great interest in madness. I am convinced that art has much to do with madness and aberrations."

3. Occidental culture admires "elaborated ideas." Dubuffet thinks that "elaborated ideas" are an impoverished state of the thought process. He is interested in "the mental process at a deeper point of its roots where I am sure the sap is richer."

4. Occidental culture is fond of analysis. Dubuffet distrusts analysis. "My inclination leads me, when I want to see something really well, to regard it with its surroundings, whole.... If there is a tree in the country, I don't bring it into my laboratory to look at it under my microscope. Because I think the wind which blows through its leaves is necessary for knowledge of the tree and cannot be separated from it...."

5. "... our culture is based on an enormous confidence in language — especially the written language, and the belief in its ability to translate and elaborate thought." Dubuffet prefers the spoken to the written word. "Speech is more concrete, animated by the sound of the voice, intonations, a cough, even grimaces and mimicry, and it seems to me more effective..." Painting is more effective still than the written word, particularly painting which seeks to capture the underground and primal stages of thought.

6. The notions of beauty and ugliness are occidental concepts, unknown to primitive peoples. The notion of beauty is specious. Western man cannot agree on what is, in fact, beautiful. It would be desirable to get rid of this notion and teach men that all objects may be sources "of fascination and illumination."

In conclusion, Dubuffet states:

> *I don't find the function of assembling colors in pleasing arrangements very noble. If painting were only that, I should not lose one hour of my time in this activity.... Painting operates, through signs which are not abstract and incorporeal like words. The signs of painting are much closer to the objects themselves. Furthermore, painting manipulates materials which are themselves living substances. That is why painting allows one to go much further than words do in approaching things.*

It is peculiar to painting that it can, at will, conjure things more or less; in other words, with more or less presence, or at different stages between being and non-being.

Finally, painting can conjure things—not in isolation—but linked to all that surrounds them; a great many things simultaneously.

Painting is a more immediate and direct vehicle than verbal language, much closer to the cry; or to the dance; that is why painting is a vehicle for expressing our inner voices which is more highly effective than that of words . . . .[5]

Prinzhorn's book encouraged Dubuffet to reject two of the most basic tenets of occidental culture: the value of categorical thought (points 1 to 5) and the notion of beauty (point 6). The Hellenic principle of *Logos,* part of our cultural heritage, comprehends consciousness of self, logical reasoning, analysis and classification, language and free (purposeful) will. Dubuffet dismissed this *Logos,* to invent his own—a *Logos* (ironically so-called) which posits a moving and unoriented continuum as the only basis for our knowledge. According to this *Logos,* all things are relative, equal and subject to change. Without categories, it is without given values and hierarchies; the concepts of true and false, beautiful and ugly, real and unreal do not exist.[6]

It would be impossible not to evoke certain parallels with Surrealism at this point. In the twenties, Dubuffet was personally close to many of the Surrealists, and it is probable that a number of conceptual seeds were planted in his mind at that time. The Surrealists similarly considered categorical thought an impoverished aspect of the true workings of the mind. As André Breton stated in the *Second Surrealist Manifesto* of 1930: "There is every reason to believe that there exists a point in the mind where life and death, the real and the imaginary, the past and the future, the communicable and the non-communicable, the above and the below, cease to be perceived as contradictions. It would be vain to seek in Surrealist activity another motivation than the determination of this point."[7]

For the Surrealists, automatism would open the doors to the true process of thought. Breton defined Surrealism itself as automatism: "SURREALISM. noun, masculine. Pure psychic automatism by which one proposes to express either verbally, in writing or by any other vehicle, the real functioning of the mind."[8]

5. Dubuffet's speech *Anticultural Positions* was given in Chicago on December 20, 1951. The original English text has been published several times, most recently in *Dubuffet and the Anticulture,* Richard L. Feigen & Co., New York, 1969. The French translation (by the artist, 1963) is published in *Prospectus,* vol. I, pp. 94-100.

6. Dubuffet set forth these ideas on his *Logos* in a letter to Arnold Glimcher dated September 15, 1969 (published in *Jean Dubuffet, Simulacres,* The Pace Gallery, New York, 1969), and in a note dated March 9, 1970 (published in *Jean Dubuffet, Le Cabinet Logologique,* Centre National d'Art Contemporain, Paris, 1970).

7. André Breton, *Manifestes du surréalisme,* Jean-Jacques Pauvert, Paris, 1962, p. 154.

8. In the First Surrealist Manifesto, *Ibid.,* p. 40.

The Surrealists furthermore rejected the notion of art as an end in itself. Breton said in *Les Pas perdus:* "It would be an error to consider art as an end . . . . painting, for example should not have for its end the pleasure of the eyes. . . . I persist in believing that a picture or sculpture is justifiable only insofar as it is capable of advancing our abstract knowledge properly speaking."[9]

Dubuffet never aligned himself with the movement and the point of non-contradiction which he sought was quite different from theirs. What the Surrealists sought was an exceptional state of poetic consciousness, producing hallucinatory images of sur-reality, most of which occurred at the verbal level. Dubuffet's objective was neither sur-reality nor so-called objectivity but what one might call trans-subjectivity: the visions and delusions of an ordinary un-selfconscious subjectivity, situated at a level of the pre-verbal unconscious.

A secondary effect of Dubuffet's exposure to Prinzhorn was the constitution of a collection of what he called *Art Brut.* Prinzhorn had a collection of the art of the mentally ill which Dubuffet visited in Heidelberg many years later. His publication of case-history monographs is modeled after the case histories found in Prinzhorn's 1922 publication.

Dubuffet's collection, as he described it in 1963, consists of "works of all kinds—drawings, paintings, embroideries, modeled or sculpted figures, etc. —which present a spontaneous and strongly inventive character, as little indebted to customary art or cultural models as possible and of which the authors are obscure individuals, alien to the milieu of professional artists." It is neither naive art nor Surrealist art, both of which are merely offshoots of cultural art, but "propositions of themselves unpredictable and wholly invented both in medium (materials, techniques, etc.) and in their inspiration. . . . we require that the works considered . . . correspond to a feverish impulse and not to some episodic stimulus or caprice where exaltation plays little part."[10] Dubuffet emphasizes that it is not psychopathic art, even though more than one half of the works in the collection are by asylum patients.

It is significant that two of the sponsors of the collection when it was officially established in 1948 were André Breton and Charles Ratton.[11] In May of 1948, Dubuffet wrote to Breton:

The share which is attributed to you in the Compagnie de l'Art Brut *is yours by right, for your ideas, humors and impulses surely played a large*

9. André Breton, *Les Pas perdus,* Editions de la Nouvelle Revue Française, Paris, 1924, p. 174.

10. Dubuffet, *Prospectus,* vol. I, pp. 167-68.

11. Founded in September 1948 as *La Compagnie de l' Art Brut.* The other founders (with Dubuffet) were Jean Paulhan, Henri-Pierre Roché and Michel Tapié.

role in orienting our attention towards these activities, and it was only fitting that your place be set at that table; and if you had not wanted to sit down with us, your place would have remained empty, like the angel's place which is set; it would be occupied by you in our thoughts.[12]

During those months, Dubuffet and Breton made frequent visits to the flea market at the Porte de St. Ouen (the northern limits of Paris), to find objects of primitive art and *Art Brut.* The two were drawn to primitive art as an art that escapes the canons of classical Western culture. They saw in it a vitalism and an identification with natural forces which they found lacking in occidental art. Breton also had a lasting interest in the art of the insane. In another letter dated August 9, 1948,[13] Dubuffet mentions an article to appear in the *Cahiers de la Pléiade* in which Breton was to discuss madness and "expose his point of view which is also mine that there is no such thing as madness and that the insane *(les fous)* are no more insane than the sane *(les non-fous)* . . ."

Charles Ratton was the leading authority on primitive art in Paris. He furthermore was one of Dubuffet's earliest supporters. It was he who recommended Dubuffet to Pierre Matisse when the New York dealer made a post-war trip to Paris, looking for new artists.

The works Dubuffet started collecting in France and Switzerland in 1945 are the products—for the most part—of what could be called schizophrenic artists. These artists usually lived in an uninspirational, socially isolated environment; in extreme cases, an institution (such as a prison or an asylum); in others, merely an isolated province. The schizophrenic artist creates for his personal satisfaction alone. An unacknowledged and unintentional social therapy, his art is the invention and projection of a surrogate world for an oppressive world to which he cannot adapt. It becomes his reality, secreted for his personal use as a milieu in which to enact a fantasy life. Since his goal is not communication but a closed-circuit dialogue with himself (or with an imaginary audience of his own making), he is free to invent his own language, making up the rules as he goes along. This language usually contains certain constant characteristics: deranged syntax, compressed imagery, and a purely affective logic, all of which are indicative of a strongly introverted subjectivity.

Dubuffet has always believed in the superiority of the anti-social alienated artist who creates for his personal pleasure and satisfaction. In fact he believes that alienation is the condition proper to real creative activity:

12. Dubuffet, *Prospectus,* vol. II, p. 265.
13. Letter to Gaston Chaissac, *Ibid.,* vol. II, pp. 279-80.

*In our time, when the aspiration to the social is so unanimous (and
"alienation" is so decried), the creation of works of art is no longer
admitted—as a matter of fact, it is not even conceived—other than
addressed to the public, borrowing its language and aiming to conquer it
and receive its applause. That an artist may be entirely disinterested in the
public, even detest it, appears inconceivable to all. And the conditioning
of our minds is so strong and so persuasive that the artists themselves
(not only the professionals of cultural art but also those who under other
conditions would be disposed to create real works of art), escape it only
with the greatest difficulty, and unless there is a solid wall, like that of
some form of insanity, they let themselves little by little be seduced . . . .
I believe that there is an irreducible antagonism between the creation of
art and a desire to communicate with the public. That antagonism
confounds the artist; he refuses to assume the position of "alienation"
implied by the creative activity, and vainly attempts to reconcile his work
with a desire to be integrated into society and receive honors and awards
. . . Creative invention has surely no greater enemy than social order, with
all the appeals to adapt, to conform, to mimic, which social relationships
imply. Creative invention can only survive in taking the opposite stance,
refusal and impermeability.*[14]

The above comments and quotes provide insights into the sources of
Dubuffet's inspiration. Dubuffet addressed himself to the signs and symptoms
of madness as expressive of the universal creative impulse, uncontaminated
by cultural inhibitions. Ironically, it is through his extreme lucidity, self-
discipline, and single-minded convictions that he has arrived at an art form
which is in many ways close to that of madmen. It is unpredictable, ap-
parently illogical, defiant and impervious to the solicitations of socio-cultural
approbation. Art historical analysis is inapplicable to it except in negative
terms. Truly, the only way we can come to terms with Dubuffet's art is
by aligning it with *Art Brut*. "*Art Brut*" as Lawrence Alloway described
it in 1966 "does not consist of savage and simple images, the awful imagery
of a primordial mind erupting in art; on the contrary, psychotic and lay art
is more usually the product of compulsion and systematic delusion. It is not
the violence of a psychotic, which occurs in *this* world . . . that shapes his
art. On the contrary, psychotic and lay art tend to create an *alien* realm by
means of a complex self-referring system. It is an order that is closed to us,
an order with hidden co-ordinates, that characterizes *Art Brut*."[15] The task
at hand is to discover the "hidden co-ordinates" which make of Dubuffet's
production a unique form of art in the twentieth century.

14. *Ibid.*, vol. I, pp. 367-68.
15. Lawrence Alloway, "Introduction,"
Jean Dubuffet, 1962-66, The Solomon
R. Guggenheim Museum, New York,
1966, p. 18.

Dubuffet's art is the opposite of heroic. It is conceived in terms of the vision of the ordinary man, it aspires to the immediacy of the spoken word, and it rejects all art-historical models.[16] His subjects are not noble; furthermore, they are conspicuously limited. The themes of the human figure, landscapes and a third theme—the mundane object—are the recurrent subjects of his life-long activity. Within this simple iconographical framework, there are however shifts of emphasis. The human figure predominates through the mid and late forties, to be replaced by stones, tables, cows and landscapes in the fifties and early sixties. The subjects of the *Hourloupe* cycle, begun in 1962, are dominated by man-made objects: coffee pots, bottles, beds, basins, scissors. Nonetheless, a first impression of obvious subject matter is deceptive. Dubuffet has rarely painted from a model[17] or from nature. His models are residual mental images, of the same species as those of untrained artists or the artists of *Art Brut*.

By presenting the viewer with images of unaccustomed banality or crudeness, Dubuffet seeks to jolt him out of his acquired aesthetic responses. "... when one has looked at a painting of this kind, one looks at everything around one with a new refreshed eye, and one learns to see the unaccustomed and amusing side of things. When I say amusing, I do not mean solely the funny side, but also the grand, the moving and even the tragic aspects [of ordinary things]."[18] "The secret," Dubuffet has remarked in conversation, "is to do a thing badly. If you serve someone spinach that is cooked the way it should be, no one notices or remembers that they have eaten spinach. Whereas if you burn it, it shocks their taste-buds and they become immediately aware that it is burned spinach and they gain new insights into the characteristics of spinach, cooking, etc."[19]

Dubuffet's natural option in 1943 was to be a figurative artist. Abstract art was a recondite metaphor, not the popular vernacular he sought. However, to Dubuffet, the conventions of figurative art were sclerotic and semantically empty: "noble" subject matter, three-dimensional perspective space, volumetric illusion (with foreshortening and modeling), hierarchical composition (focusing on "essential" subject matter), "meaningful" color relationships and the use of a number of accepted media and techniques.

One of the dominant conventions of post-Renaissance figurative art is that of three-dimensional perspective space. The convention of perspective is, however, unknown to the *Art Brut* artist. As Dubuffet has written:

> *Effects of perspective are constantly found in the art to which we are accustomed; we are in fact so accustomed to it that we have difficulty*

16. As mentioned earlier, Dubuffet was not ignorant of art history nor blind to what was going on around him. However, it is our intention to concentrate on his relationship to *Art Brut*. This does not obviate other sources, influences, and analogies which can be found in relating Dubuffet to "cultural" phenomena such as the painters Klee, Fautrier, Léger, the writers Artaud, Queneau, Céline, to mention only a few.

17. One exception is the painting of 1944, *Gardes du corps* (cat. no. 2) where Dubuffet used a professional male model.

18. Dubuffet, *Prospectus*, vol. I, p. 47.

19. In conversation with the author, January 31, 1972.

understanding images which are organized according to another principle . . . But ordinary art depicts the perceived world . . . . Whereas . . . mental space does not resemble three-dimensional perceived space and has no use for notions such as above or below, in front of or behind, close or distant. [Mental space] presents itself as flowing, whirling, meandering water and therefore its transcription requires entirely different devices from those deemed appropriate for transcribing the perceived world.[20]

Since 1943, Dubuffet's paintings emphasize a two-dimensional surface. In paintings where the figure predominates—between 1943 and 1950—it exists in a variety of complex relationships to the surrounding space or ground, none of which allows any illusion of overlapping or depth. For example, in *Danseuse de corde* (cat. no. 4), the flattened silhouette of the rope-skipper is interlaced in an uninterrupted pattern of line and color. In other paintings of 1944, the figure is as though cut out and placed on a uniform or patterned field. In the *Macadam* series and the portraits of 1945-47, some figures are incised into thick impasto, whereas others are built up on it. The *Grotesque Landscapes* of 1949 are animated by transparent line drawings whereas the *Corps de dames* series of 1950-51 presents drastically flattened effigies which are sometimes bled into the surrounding field. At all times, the space is defined as a two-dimensional surface, a deliberate option on the part of the artist:

> *The objective of painting is to animate a surface which is by definition two-dimensional and without depth. One does not enrich it in seeking effects of relief or trompe-l'oeil through shading; one denatures and adulterates it . . . . Let us seek instead ingenious ways to flatten objects on the surface; and let the surface speak its own language and not an artificial language of three-dimensional space which is not proper to it . . . . I feel the need to leave the surface visibly flat. My eyes like to rest on a surface which is very flat, particularly a rectangular surface. The objects represented will be transformed into pancakes, as though flattened by a pressing iron.*[21]

During the next decade, when the human image is less central, spatial depth and relief are consistently absent. One of the artist's more frequent themes—the table—is conceived as a four-legged two-dimensional shape. Ironically, Cézanne's "tilted" table-tops are recalled by the culturally-conditioned eye. Dubuffet's tables, however, are pushed to an illogical extreme. They are not the depicted illusion of a three-dimensional reality, but tables as "seen" in the irrational mind's eye.

20. Dubuffet, *Prospectus*, vol. I, pp. 447-48.
21. *Ibid.*, vol. I, p. 74.

Landscapes, an increasingly prevalent theme, are similarly tipped, flattened and fitted to the rectangular frame. When they are inhabited by figures, the relationship of figure to ground is rarely one of surface to depth. In some cases the figure has no substance; it is seared into the landscape (*La Chèvre égarée,* cat. no. 62). In others such as the *Tableaux d'assemblages* of 1955-57 (*La Pointe au pitre,* cat. no. 86), figure and ground appear to be cut from a single fabric and reassembled, like a patchwork quilt. The horizon line, when it exists, functions as a decorative border, not as a demarcation evoking outlying space. Sometimes the "sky" has more physical substance than the "earth" which exists as a mentally animated void. By 1958, all spatial separations have disappeared and Dubuffet's mental landscape stretches from edge to edge, creating an uninterrupted unified pattern.

Nonetheless the indication of identifiable subjects or objects in the paintings prior to 1962 tempts the viewer to project a figure-ground reading on these two-dimensional surfaces. Through cultural habit, he imagines a disparity between a three-dimensional subject and a two-dimensional depiction and injects illusions of relief or volume where none are intended. The *Hourloupe* cycle, begun in 1962, precludes this reading. The large early *Hourloupe* paintings illustrate a concept of all-over design which in America we identify with Jackson Pollock. Dubuffet's articulation of the all-over surface, however, is quite different in its sources and its elaboration from that of American Abstract Expressionism.

As William Rubin has pointed out, Pollock's rhythmic network of gestures is close in form and feeling to Analytical Cubist "scaffolding."[22] In Pollock's mature drip paintings, one is conscious of a positive-negative superposition in the figure-ground tracery which permits a shifting from surface to depth and back, and an illusion of an opening and closing of the field determined by human impulse. Dubuffet's *Hourloupe* paintings present none of these illusions. The surface is hermetically sealed, a jig-saw-like mosaic of tightly interlocking cellular forms. Each form is closed and of a piece; yet, as in Pollock, the system is self-generating.

Perhaps the basic difference lies in the fact that Dubuffet's imagery refers to another level of human discourse: that of the even monotonous flux of the irrational or pre-logical mind. His formal equations are uninterrupted, nonfocused, barely articulated. In humanist terms, they are situated at the edge of non-expression, non-being, nothingness. They open onto what Dubuffet calls "anti-life", which "is not death [but] something else again."[23]

22. William Rubin, "Toward a Critical Framework," *Artforum,* Los Angeles, 1966, vol. V, no. 1, p. 55.
23. Dubuffet, *Prospectus,* vol. II, p. 379.

The *Hourloupe* cycle reflects the culmination of Dubuffet's pictorial ambitions. The form adopted for the *Hourloupe* paintings, said Dubuffet in 1969, is

> *that of an uninterrupted and resolutely uniform meandering script, (unifying all planes to the frontal plane, paying no heed to the particular space of the object described, neither its dimensions, nor its distance nor closeness) thereby abolishing all particularities, all categories (by which I mean the usual classifications adopted by our reflexive mind which makes distinctions between one notion and another: between the notion of* chair *for example and that of* tree, *that of* human figure, cloud, ground, landscape, *or anything else) so that this consistently uniform script indifferently applied to all things (and it should be emphasized, not only visible objects but also invisible inventions of our thoughts, imagination or fantasy; mixed together without discrimination) will reduce them all to the lowest common denominator and restitute a continuous undifferentiated universe; it will thereby dissolve the categories which our mind habitually employs to decipher (better to say to cipher) the facts and spectacles of the world. Herewith the circulation of the mind from one object to another, from one category to another will be liberated and its mobility greatly increased.*[24]

To sum it up, Dubuffet says one paragraph later, "my operation is to erase all categories and regress toward an undifferentiated continuum."

This text is crucial to the understanding of Dubuffet's pictorial priorities. The elimination of the categories of rational thought translates pictorially into a suppression of differentiated planes, hierarchical composition, color as value, and other traditional aspects of the work of art as it exists in Western culture.

Obviously, Dubuffet would have to shun illusionism in terms of foreshortening and modeling. Yet an equivocation between what is reality and what is illusion—such as is generally found in figurative painting—persists. Usually this form of equivocation arises from a tension in the viewer's mind between an absent reality and an illusion which is present. But Dubuffet reverses these terms. What is present is a concrete presence or reality. What is absent is an illusion or mental image which served as the model for the concrete reality now before the viewer.

The term which qualifies this kind of ambiguity is the French word *simulacre*, a term the artist chose for one specific phase of his activity: the black and white sculptures of 1969. As the artist explained in the same letter

24. Letter to Arnold Glimcher, see fn. 6.

26

of 1969, [25] the French word *simulacre* signifies *une apparence sensible qui se donne pour une réalité,* or a physical (sensuous) presence which proposes itself as a reality. The example Dubuffet selects is that of ghosts or apparitions. Ghosts appear as real presences when in fact they are figments of the viewer's imagination. Dubuffet's images, although endowed with an undeniable concrete presence, are in fact the transcription of illusions. Concrete reality is not their source. They are deliberate delusions to which the artist has given shape, substance, form and presence.

Although in the letter quoted above, the artist is describing one specific phase of his activity, his remarks elucidate not only the form but the content of his life's work. These three-dimensional works, says Dubuffet, "are endowed with an equivocal status, which produces a wavering in the mind between the function of material objects and that of immaterial figurations of objects." He continues, saying that although these objects address themselves to the viewer in the form of three-dimensional objects, they are in fact pure mental evocations. Their materiality is specious. Their objecthood is fallacious. They are the mere materializations of mental operations. They cannot be considered sculpture; rather they should be considered three-dimensional painting, which is to say they are three-dimensional illusions. The artist also considered calling these works "mental derivatives endowed with physical substance" but discarded this as too unwieldy.

Dubuffet's process is the realist painter's process in reverse. Starting from an illusion, he invents a physical reality. Dubuffet has compared this process to a "sausage-machine run backwards." "Many artists begin with the pig and make sausages. I begin with sausages from which I reconstitute a pig."[26]

Thus, a painting of a coffee pot (cat. no. 133) is the embodiment of an idea of a coffee pot; a *matériologie* is the interpretation of a mental landscape (cat. nos. 112-115); a *portrait* is the depiction of a conceptualization of a friend (cat. nos. 25-32). In a deliberate attempt to confound the viewer, these "mental derivatives" are endowed with a strong physical presence.

Sustained contradictions between the imaginary and the literal are characteristic of *Art Brut*. Dubuffet saw this in one of the artists in his collection: "Every aspect reflects a flagrant desire on the part of the artist to confer not a physical but a mental character to these images; however simultaneously the artist's heavy lines, and his choice of harmonious and powerful coloring reflect the aim to endow the site with a strongly convincing physical presence." [27]

25. *Ibid.*
26. In conversation with the author, December 8, 1972.
27. *Publications de la Compagnie de l'Art Brut,* fascicule 4, Paris, 1965, p. 117.

The *Corps de dames* series of 1950-51 offers a group of examples where the equivocation between a conceptualization and physical substance is eloquently projected. At first contact, the viewer is assaulted by an effect of flagellated, or disintegrating, smeared or bruised flesh. He is as though confronted with his own desecrated body. The impact of a visceral exposure of flesh is achieved through the combined aspects of the indeterminate configuration of the image and the surface which abounds with haptic incident. Most of the figures are close to flesh color; yet the wine-colored tints which generally predominate endow the bodies with an unhealthy aura of imminent decay.

One cannot remain indifferent to these images; yet one never succumbs to the illusion that these are real human entities. As subjects, they have no psychological presence; as objects, their physical volume is reduced to a flattened skin pinioned to the canvas. Nonetheless, they elicit a violently physical response. Dubuffet has given concrete shape and substance to a generalized concept of femaleness. It is the substantiation of that idea which has trespassed into the world of our experience.

Similar responses and incongruities are found in relation to the series of 1951-52: *Landscaped Tables, Landscapes of the Mind, Stones of Philosophy*. Despite the heavy impasto of these paintings—in which the relief is sometimes highlighted by a glistening varnish—the titles indicate that these are metaphysical images.

In the *Hourloupe* paintings, such physical-mental contradictions are attenuated. The flat vinyl surface of these works does not address itself to the viewer as a physical presence but as a transcription of the oscillations of the pre-reflexive psyche. Furthermore, the elimination of natural and associative colors reinforces the character of these works as landscapes of the mind.

It is conceivable that Dubuffet progressed from the radically flat *Hourloupe* paintings into three-dimensional works for reasons related to the preceding discussion. Paintings such as *Fusil canardier* (cat. no. 134) or *Cuisinière à gaz*, as unequivocal mental images, cannot be confused with physical entities.[28] However, the translation of these fantasy constructs into three-dimensional objects amplifies the illusion-reality conflict to an unprecedented degree. As Dubuffet stated:

It is perhaps in the chair series that I have most felt the discomfort resulting from the confusion of an object with its figuration. What I mean is when the configuration of an object becomes an object itself. A painter who depicts a chair on a flat canvas does not fear for a moment that his

28. These works belong to Dubuffet's series of *ustensiles utopiques* or imaginary, functionless utensils.

depiction will be taken for a real chair, or, in other terms, that his evocation of a chair will slip from the world of evocations into the world of existing objects, objects susceptible in turn to give rise to evocations. One would never entertain the idea of sitting on a chair depicted on a canvas whereas if the same chair depiction is produced in three dimensions and thereby given volume by the sculptor, one would be tempted to do so. When I say given volume, I mean given attributes which liken it to real objects, before which the mind is confounded and reacts to it not as the transcription of a movement of the mind responding to an object but simply as an object belonging to the perceptual world. It no longer belongs to the world of the mind but belongs to the physical world, not to say the functional world—the world of chairs on which one sits . . . .

The very particular point (point of the mind I mean) where an equivocation between the imaginary and the real arises, that point between the domain of evocations and that of objects, posing the greatest threat of slipping from one to the other, that point produces in me uneasiness and discomfort but at the same time it exerts a fascination over me to the point of not knowing if I fear it or if I seek it out and solicit it.[29]

Dubuffet's most recent series, the *praticables*, is an extension of this idea. A *praticable*, or practical, is a kind of theater prop: a real object (such as a telephone) divested of its real functions, to become the representation of that object on the stage. Thus, throughout his career, Dubuffet has created situations of extreme perceptual instability and intellectual uneasiness disguised in terms of the utmost banality.

In his endeavor to dismantle the edifice of categorical thought and to celebrate the aberrations of the pre-reflexive mind, perspective and illusionism are only two of the filters which Dubuffet shatters. A third one is composition: an acquired discipline based on value judgments, analysis and synthesis, and implying a movement toward self-determination and communication. The schizophrenic artist ignores these premises. In contrast to the common visual syntax of professional artists, his idiom is loosely structured according to the most elementary human patterns: isolation, serial repetition, vertical stacking, chaotic accumulation, frontality and symmetry.

Dubuffet, like all "unexceptional" Frenchmen who have been through the French educational system, had a mind inherently structured by the axioms of Cartesian analysis. Yet in his *Anticultural Positions*,[30] he expressed his distrust of value judgments and analysis. In his work, the distinctions

29. In a "note to Max Loreau on the painted styrofoams of the *Hourloupe* cycle" dated July 5, 1969, and published in *Jean Dubuffet, L'Hourloupe,* Kunsthalle Basel, 1970.
30. See fn. 5.

between what exists and what does not, between reality and non-reality, between thinking and feeling, perceiving and imagining are deliberately blurred. Figures float and tilt, upside down and sideways, filling the frame of the canvas whose flat planar surface is the only space they respect. There is no acknowledgment of external-world concepts such as gravity. Accepted pictorial premises—relationships of figure to ground, figure to figure, part to whole, whole to part, harmony, contrast, tensions—are equally ignored. So that the pictorial problems and solutions produced by the "artistic" manipulation of these principles are boldly lacking throughout Dubuffet's work.

Whereas the notion of compositional structure is never inborn, a color sense, although in large part conditioned, appears to have some innate basis. Dubuffet has always had a highly developed color sense, despite his efforts to obliterate it. In 1946, when Pierre Matisse had just become Dubuffet's New York dealer, he showed some paintings to his father in Paris. Henri Matisse looked at them with a puzzled expression. After a long pause, he said: "I do not understand what it is all about, but he has an extraordinary sense of color." He added, "And it's a very French sensibility."[31]

Clearly, in 1946 (at the age of forty-five), Dubuffet was still a victim of his "educated" sensibility. The paintings bear this out. Starting in 1943, Dubuffet launched an attack on good taste. As such, it was largely unsuccessful. The paintings of 1943-44 are pleasing. They are almost facile in their appeal as compared to the varied degrees of repugnance which Dubuffet's successive cycles of work have inspired. Since his aims were obviously incompatible with his personal instincts, Dubuffet resorted to material such as gravel, cement, Swedish putty, sand (and at other times leaves, bark, banana peels, butterfly wings), which would impose their own natural hues. Elsewhere he worked with distemper, glazes, emulsions, plastic paints, zinc oxide and resin varnishes. These media, spilling into one another, clotting, bleeding, coalescing, created their own chromatic mixtures and color interaction.

Despite these experiments, Dubuffet was still unsuccessful. No matter how the artist sought to stifle his color impulses, prior to 1962 and the *Hourloupe* series, his color is consistently sensuous and appealing. It is direct in its expression, subtle in its variations, supremely evocative and largely unexpected, due to its dependence on unprecedented materials. We cannot—nor do we wish to—remain indifferent to Dubuffet's color, and its psychic power and visual effects are such that they are obviously the products of human decision.

31. Recounted by Pierre Matisse in conversation with the author, November 15, 1972.

So that the *Hourloupe* series represents the ultimate solution: an arbitrary restriction of the palette to red, white, blue and black, and, concurrently, a complete disaffection for natural or the imitation of natural materials, with their subtle values and associations. Since Dubuffet rarely used flat primary colors prior to that time, this choice appears as a deliberate substitution. This palette, which one can conjecture ran counter to his innate sensibility, surely corresponded to new priorities. Red and blue, as used here, are neutral colors lacking in associative power; the function of color in the *Hourloupe* paintings is as unevocative and non-expressionist as the continuum of ciphers—or visual equation—that graphically articulates their surfaces.

The bright or brutal colors of Dubuffet's earlier work simultaneously enhanced and denied the reality of the image. The result was an evocative— both real and elusive—imagery such as the subjective mind secretes. The function of color in the *Hourloupe* cycle is quite different. Since from the outset, the *Hourloupe* imagery is more radically removed from the perceptual world, color serves to project and determine abstract conceits in visual terms, according to a closed, non-associational, self-referring system. In other words, the injection of primary color in flat planes or striations gives immediate and literal presence and substance to what are essentially pure "mental derivatives."

Dubuffet's initial approach to materials was founded on the idea that conventional techniques inspire conventional imagery whereas unaccustomed non-art instruments, supports and media stimulate the mind to unprecedented adventures. A fundamental characteristic of *Art Brut* is a dependence on "materials of fortune." In his compulsive need to project and create images, the schizophrenic artist adopts any medium at hand. "Materials of fortune" are literally anything. The repertory found at *La Compagnie de l'Art Brut* includes leaves, volcanic stone, pumice, cement, sea-shells, leather, string, bread, vegetable peels, coal, glass shards. Tools range from a spoon handle to a ball-point pen; supports include the wood paneling of a room, wrapping paper, blotting paper, fabrics.

The notion that any and all materials may serve the cause of popular art appealed to Dubuffet. Although oil paint was Dubuffet's most common vehicle between 1943 and 1962, he transformed it, creating emulsions, thickening it with sand and glue to an opaque and gritty paste, and consistently defiling its traditional identity. At other times, Dubuffet resorted to extraneous materials such as tar, gravel, lime, plaster, asphalt, even mud.

According to Dubuffet's definition, art, like life, is accident-prone. All men are artists; all products of the creative urge fall under the heading of art. The artist is not a demiurge but an ordinary human being; he is thereby susceptible to the vicissitudes of fortune that that implies:

> ... the artist is harnessed to fortune; (art) is not a dance to be danced alone, but as a couple; fortune is the partner. It pulls one way, while the artist guides it as he can but with flexibility, working to take advantage of the fortuitous as it presents itself, trying to mold it to his ends, never precluding a deviation from his original goals at any moment .... It is not exactly with just any fortune that the artist is involved, but with a particular kind of fortune, indigenous to the material employed. The term fortune is inexact. Better to speak of the inclinations and aspirations of the medium as it resists his hand.
>
> It is a duet between the artist and his medium. Each must speak freely and directly and visibly his own language. One must allow all the fortunes proper to the material to emerge ... To try to prevent these vagaries of fortune would be to deprive the work of all vitality.[32]

Dubuffet invited accidents; he courted chance. He consented to what others would correct as errors. As Max Jacob, one of his early mentors, said, "Error alone is fertile."[33] In the extreme cases of the *Matériologies* and the *Texturologies,* of 1957-60, the mind and hand of the artist appear to play no role at all. Some of his titles such as *La Vie sans l'homme* ("Life without Man") are descriptive of a painting *and* a psychic state. There remains no visible trace of the passage of a reflexive mind. The protagonist is "matter."

The *Hourloupe* series was born of doodlings with a ball-point pen. Conceived as proliferating mental imagery, the success of the *Hourloupe* depends on the absence of immediate sensuous allusions. As Lawrence Alloway pointed out in 1966: "... in place of the emphases possible with a split nib, the succession of pauses and replenishments, the ball-point gives a hard, unaccented, continuous line. In 1964 the drawings with markers develop the unaccented line further; the evenly plump track of a felt pen, strongly but softly, produces a quasi-streamline."[34]

Ball-point pens and markers (or felt-tipped pens) are modern man's most pedestrian writing utensils. Thus an impersonal anonymous medium gave rise to Dubuffet's most depersonalized and generalized ideational forms.

32. Dubuffet, *Prospectus*, vol. I, pp. 58-59.
33. Quoted by Dubuffet in a letter, *Ibid.*, vol. II, p. 233.
34. Lawrence Alloway, *op. cit.*, p. 16.

Dubuffet's generation is characterized by disenchantment. The artists and philosophers who came of age after World War II looked for alternatives to an idealistic humanism conceived as inappropriate to the modern world. God being dead, man discovered himself critically alone, responsible to himself and to his fellow men, with no traditional beliefs to guide his life. As Bergson and Freud were among their spiritual mentors, an acknowledgement of the powers of the unconscious in determining man's relations to the world is also important to understanding their spiritual positions. Since man's real substance is his psychic life—a moving flux of undetermined impulses—to define him as a prime mover of the universe appeared as erroneous a claim as the medieval belief that the earth was flat. On the contrary, the universe moves, forms and finally qualifies man. So that the role of individual responsibility (and the question of personal identity) in this interplay of forces had to be reassessed.

Sartre believed that man can determine his identity through his acts. Camus (who occupies a transitional position between Existential and Post-Existential thought) took a more skeptical stance. Questioning the myths that man is good or free, he inferred that man's motivations are not naturally noble or meaningful. And, although responsible only to himself, he is nonetheless imprisoned in an inextricable network of relationships with others which greatly determines his behavior. Camus saw man as neither pawn nor hero but as anti-hero, existing somewhere between these poles. Neither totally dependent on outside forces, nor totally responsible, he is only *relatively* responsible.

The delicate balance which Camus portrayed between man's free will and the contradictory fabric of his existence was subsequently tipped to a more pessimistic perspective. Post-Existential artists like Beckett and Ionesco see the environment in which we live as destructive of any will to act. Their anti-hero exists as a *simulacre:* an abstract cipher parading in the guise of man. He interprets events as the fruits of his own initiative when it is obvious they are not. He moves or is moved . . . toward nothing in particular. He speaks . . . in empty clichés. As Dubuffet has said in another context, his reality is specious, his objecthood is fallacious.[35] Yet this is the configuration of modern man: a diffuse presence of humors and psychic states with no evident identity.

The parallels with Dubuffet's art are obvious. His landscapes are undetermined fragments of space and time in which the waves and eddies of

35. See page 27 here.

subjective thought confront the external forces of materials. His objects, discovered out of context, are emptied of their accustomed specificity. His human figures are without motion or expression; they are nameless ciphers of man.

Throughout Dubuffet's work extreme psychic isolation is portrayed. The objects of his perception are bound by no determined relationships either in time (sequence) or in space (to surface, depth, center, edge) or to other figures. Their positioning is arbitrary; they may be moved from place to place. Their scale may be altered without affecting the whole. If identity is defined as a convergence of specific relationships, clearly Dubuffet paints nonentities.

The fortuitous placement of perceptual objects in a field is found consistently in Dubuffet's art. It is explicitly visible in the *Assemblages d'empreintes* (1953-54) and the *Tableaux d' assemblages* (1955-57). The works in these two groups were arrived at through the random cutting and assembling of textured surfaces, surfaces also prepared at random. In reference to these series, Dubuffet has expressed his satisfaction at being able to shift and displace images before fixing them with glue.[36] In his current work, the *praticables,* his freedom is even greater, and again it was the problem of distributing figures in a visual field which inspired this solution. "I conceived the *praticables,*" he related in conversation, "in order to create free figures and independent grounds and subsequently assemble them in any combination."[37] In the three series mentioned, the figures and their environment are of identical substance: spattered India ink in the *Assemblages d'empreintes,* maculated canvas in the *Tableaux d'assemblages,* a continuous chain of cellular forms in the *praticables.* As a result, no matter how it is placed, the figure does not function as an additive or relational component. Visually it dissolves or locks itself into a continuous formal and textural fabric.

Dubuffet's anti-relational imagery translates a freedom from hierarchical imperatives, a freedom won at the expense of composition, illusionism, perspective, color interaction, in a word, at the expense of "art" as his generation knew it. Psychologically, it was achieved by observing madness or the disintegration of categorical thought. Like the *Art Brut* artists he admires, Dubuffet freely constitutes celebrations, based on delusions, which he offers as an alternative to everyday life. Yet beneath the surface of the *simulacres, praticables* and mirages, there exists an undercurrent of tragic humanism, a tragic vision of the helpless anonymity of modern man.

36. Dubuffet, *Prospectus,* vol. II, pp. 116-17.
37. With the author, December 8, 1972.

Remarks on the Unveiling of The Group of Four Trees, New York, October 24, 1972

Jean Dubuffet

translated by Benita Eisler

At this time I should like to offer a few explanatory remarks about the monument whose installation we are celebrating today.

Obviously, the work stands in full view of everyone here and each of us must now look at it with his own eyes and bring to it his own associations. My own belief is that a work of art fails in its function if its meaning is too limited. I believe that the meaning, or rather the *meanings,* of any work of art should be wide open so that each of us can absorb it into our own particular universe. (I am referring, of course, to our mental universe.)

With your permission, I should like to offer a few guidelines to the aims and mental processes which guided my hand in the conception of this monument.

This sculpture forms part of a cycle of my works to which I have given the name *L'Hourloupe,* and which was begun in 1962, or ten years ago.

I should mention in passing that *L'Hourloupe* is a word whose invention was based upon its sound. In French, these sounds suggest some wonderland or grotesque object or creature, while at the same time they evoke something rumbling and threatening with tragic overtones. Both are implied.

In my thinking, the works that belong to the *Hourloupe* cycle are linked one to the other, each of them an element destined to become part of the whole. The cycle itself is conceived as the figuration of a world other than our own or, if you prefer, parallel to ours, and it is this world which bears the name *l'Hourloupe.*

The works originating in this cycle are in the form of sinuous graphisms responding with immediacy to spontaneous and, so to speak, uncontrolled impulses of the hand which traces them. Within these graphisms, imprecise, fugitive and ambiguous figures take shape. Their movement sets off in the observer's mind a hyperactivation of the visionary faculty. In these interlacings all kinds of objects form and dissolve as the eyes scan the surface, linking intimately the transitory and the permanent, the real and the fallacious. The result (at least, this is the way it works for me) is an awareness of the illusory character of the world which we think of as real, and to which we give the name of the real world. These graphisms, with their constantly shifting references, have the virtue (to me, I should add again) of challenging the legitimacy of what we habitually accept as reality. This reality is, in truth, only one option collectively adopted, to interpret the world around us—

one option among an infinity of equally legitimate possibilities. Had any one of these other options been adopted at the dawn of human thought, it would today offer the same impression of reality that we now confer upon the established one. Thus, as you can see, a philosophic humor presides over the works of the *Hourloupe* cycle—introducing a doubt about the true materiality of the everyday world. It too may be only a mental construct.

At the beginning, this cycle included only drawings and paintings. Subsequently, I wished to give them greater corporality. I undertook to assimilate them to three-dimensional forms, presenting, as do all solids, several sides to the observer. The result was objects of equivocal status. They have been called painted sculptures, but this term is not really accurate. Rather, they should be considered drawings which extend and expand in space.

I then desired to endow these unleashed graphisms, these lines escaped from the flat sheet of their usual support, with monumental dimensions.

I could not have hoped for a place better suited to this monument,

austerely intellectual in concept, than the plaza where it stands today, a site richly distinguished by the high intensity activities which take place here. Its specific character—in another sense, to be sure, and in other directions, but with unquestionably as much authority and, I would even say, poetry—symbolizes with impressive force, the effectiveness of human thought. Indeed, this plaza, and the prodigious buildings which rise above and surround it, are the dramatic illustration of an extraordinary celebration of reason, logic and calculation.

I do not believe that these four trees, which I hope will not be taken as representations of real trees but as semblances of the thrust and fertility of human thought, bear contradiction in any way to the site upon which they now stand. Indeed, in their capricious and aberrant graphisms, they give an impression—and this was intentional—of feverish intoxication. But they seem to me, by this same febrility, to manifest the ardent source of the enormous intellectual machinery of which this plaza is the core.

I confess to being deeply moved that New York, this city so marvelously welcoming and marvelously eager to embrace every bold intellectual innovation, fearlessly accepted this allegory.

Elocution faite à l'occasion de l'inauguration du groupe des quatre arbres

Jean Dubuffet

Je voudrais maintenant donner quelques indications sur le monument dont nous fêtons ici aujourd'hui l'érection.

Il est bien vrai qu'il s'offre aux yeux de tous et chacun doit maintenant le regarder avec ses propres yeux et ses propres associations d'esprit. Je crois qu'une oeuvre d'art ne remplit pas ce qui est attendu d'elle si sa signification est trop limitée. Je crois que la signification ou plutôt *les* significations d'une oeuvre d'art doivent être ouvertes largement de manière à permettre que chacun puisse la faire entrer dans son univers propre. Bien sûr, c'est son univers mental que je veux dire.

Mais c'est sur les visées de son auteur, et sur les positions d'esprit qui ont conduit sa main dans la conception de ce monument que je veux maintenant fournir, si on veut me le permettre, quelque éclaircissement.

Ce monument s'inscrit dans un cycle de mes travaux auquel j'ai donné le nom de L'Hourloupe et qui a pris naissance en 1962, c'est à dire il y a maintenant dix ans.

Je mentionnerai en passant que ce mot de L'Hourloupe est un nom inventé en fonction de sa consonance. Celle-ci, en français, évoque à la fois quelque objet ou personnage de statut féerique et grotesque, et aussi par ailleurs quelque chose de tragiquement grondant et menaçant. Les deux ensemble.

Dans ma pensée les travaux rattachés à ce cycle de L'Hourloupe sont liés les uns aux autres, chacun d'eux étant un élément destiné à s'insérer dans l'ensemble. Celui-ci veut être la figuration d'un monde autre que le nôtre, un monde, si l'on veut, parallèle au nôtre, et c'est ce monde qui porte le nom de L'Hourloupe.

Mes travaux procédant de ce cycle mettent en oeuvre des graphismes sinueux répondant avec immédiateté à des impulsions spontanées et, pour ainsi dire, non contrôlées, de la main qui les trace. Dans ces graphismes s'amorcent des figurations incertaines, fugaces, ambiguës. Leur mouvement déclenche dans l'esprit de qui se trouve en leur présence une suractivation de la faculté de visionner dans leurs lacis toutes sortes d'objets qui se font et se défont à mesure que le regard se transporte, liant ainsi intimement le transitoire et le permanent, le réel et le fallacieux. Il en résulte — du moins est-ce ainsi que cela fonctionne pour moi — une prise de conscience du caractère illusoire du monde que nous croyons réel, auquel nous donnons le nom de monde réel. Ces graphismes aux références constamment ambiguës ont la vertu — elles l'ont pour moi, veux-je toujours dire — de mettre en question le bien-fondé de ce que nous avons coutume de regarder comme réalité et qui n'est en vérité qu'une option collectivement adoptée pour interpréter le monde qui nous entoure parmi une infinité d'autres options tout autres, qui ne seraient ni moins ni plus légitimes. Si l'une ou l'autre de ces autres options avait été adoptée à l'aube de la pensée, elle nous donnerait aujourd'hui la même impression de réalité que nous donne celle qui s'est trouvée prévaloir. Comme vous le voyez donc, préside à ces travaux du cycle de L'Hourloupe une humeur philosophique... introduisant un doute dans la vraie matérialité du monde auquel nous avons journellement affaire. Il pourrait bien n'être qu'une création de notre pensée.

Ces travaux dans leur début recouraient seulement à des dessins et peintures. Il est advenu que j'ai ensuite éprouvé le désir de leur donner plus de corporalité. J'ai entrepris de les associer à des formes tridimensionnelles et offrant donc au regard, comme tout solide, plusieurs côtés. Il en est résulté des objets de statut équivoque. On les a désignés sous le terme de sculptures peintes mais cette expression est un peu erronée. C'est plutôt de dessins s'élançant et s'expansant dans l'espace qu'il faut parler.

Le désir m'est venu alors de donner à ces graphismes déchaînés, à ces graphismes s'échappant de la feuille plane qui leur sert habituellement de support, des dimensions monumentales.

Je ne pouvais pas espérer, pour y ériger un monument revêtu de ce statut austèrement mental, un lieu mieux adapté à l'y voir érigé que n'est cette place où je le vois aujourd'hui, si fortement dotée elle-même—dans son aspect, dans les activités de haute tension qui s'y exercent—d'un caractère qui, d'une autre manière, il est vrai, par de toutes autres voies, mais avec autant d'autorité sans doute, et, dirai-je aussi, de poésie, symbolise avec une intensité saisissante les efficiences de la pensée. Dans cette place en effet et dans l'ensemble des édifices prodigieux qui la surplombent et l'avoisinent se voit dramatisée une extraordinaire fête qui est celle de la raison, de la logique et du calcul.

Il ne me semble pas que ces quatre arbres, dont je souhaite qu'ils soient reçus non comme des images de vrais arbres mais comme des semblances des élancements et arborescences de la pensée, portent contradiction au site où ils sont maintenant placés. Ils ont en effet, et je l'ai voulu ainsi, avec leurs graphismes capricieux et aberrants, une allure d'ivresse enfiévrée. Mais ils me semblent, par cet enfièvrement même, manifester la source brûlante de l'énorme machinerie intellectuelle dont ce site est le coeur.

Je suis fort ému que New York, la ville merveilleusement accueillante et merveilleusement éprise de toutes les hardiesses dans le domaine des novations de la pensée, n'ait pas craint cette allégorie.

Works in the exhibition

Oeuvres exposées

The following checklist is divided into four sections:

  I. Paintings, butterfly wing assemblages and small statues

  II. Works on paper including prints

  III. Illustrated books

  IV. Three-dimensional works from the *Hourloupe* cycle

In each section works are listed for the most part chronologically. However, in certain cases strict date order is not followed so as to respect the unity of groups of works based on a particular theme or executed in a single medium.

Dimensions are given in inches and centimeters; in both cases height precedes width.

The notation L. Fasc.——, fig.—— refers to the *Catalogue des travaux de Jean Dubuffet*, compiled by Max Loreau, and listed on pages 301-303.

*denotes works to be shown in New York only.

Les notices suivantes sont établies en quatre parties:

  I. Peintures, assemblages en ailes de papillons, petites statues

  II. Oeuvres sur papier, y compris les oeuvres graphiques

  III. Livres illustrés

  IV. Oeuvres à trois dimensions du cycle de l'Hourloupe

A l'intérieur de chaque partie, les sujets sont présentés par ordre chronologique. Cependant, afin de garder l'unité d'une série établie sur un seul thème ou procédé technique, il arrive quelquefois que l'ordre chronologique ne soit pas strictement suivi.

Les dimensions des oeuvres sont données en *inches* et en centimètres, dans les deux cas, la hauteur précède la largeur.

L'indication L. Fasc. ——, fig. —— renvoie au *Catalogue des travaux de Jean Duffett*, élaboré par Max Loreau. Une liste annotée des fascicules se trouve à la page 301-303.

*indique que l'oeuvre sera exposée à New York seulement.

Section I Paintings, butterfly wing
assemblages and small statues

I Peintures, assemblages en ailes
de papillons, petites statues

*1

Masques, 1935
Masks, 1935

a. Robert Polguère, papier mâché,
25 x 19 cm. (9⅞ x 7½")
b. André Claude, papier mâché,
24 x 14,5 cm. (9½ x 5⅞")
c. René Pontier, papier mâché,
28 x 17 cm. (11 x 6¾")

Collection The Hirshhorn Museum
and Sculpture Garden, Smithsonian
Institution, Washington, D.C.

L. Fasc. I, page 21.

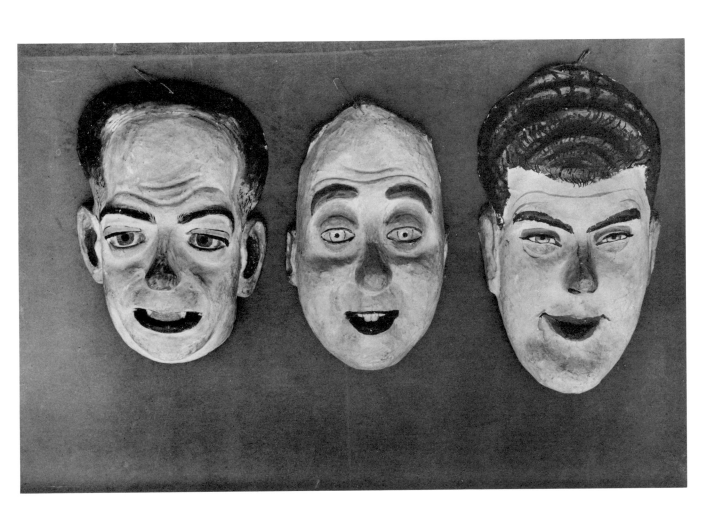

2

Gardes du corps, janvier 1943
Body Guards, January 1943

Huile sur toile, 116 x 89 cm.
Oil on canvas, 45¾ x 35″

Collection particulière

L. Fasc. I, fig. 23.

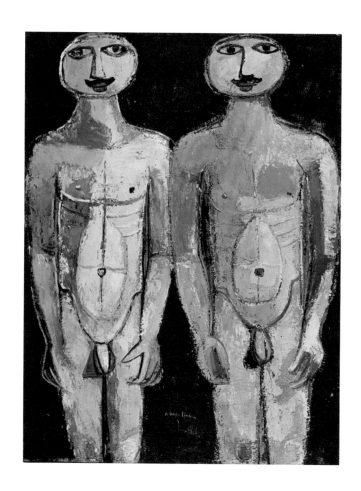

3

Petit Sergent Major, février 1943
Little Sergeant Major, February 1943

Huile sur toile, 61 x 50 cm.
Oil on canvas, 24 x 19¾"

Private Collection

L. Fasc. I, fig. 25.

4

Danseuse de corde, février 1943
Rope Skipper, February 1943

Huile sur toile, 100 x 73 cm.
Oil on canvas, 39⅜ x 28¾″

Collection Mr. and Mrs. Morton L.
Janklow, New York

L. Fasc. I, fig. 27.

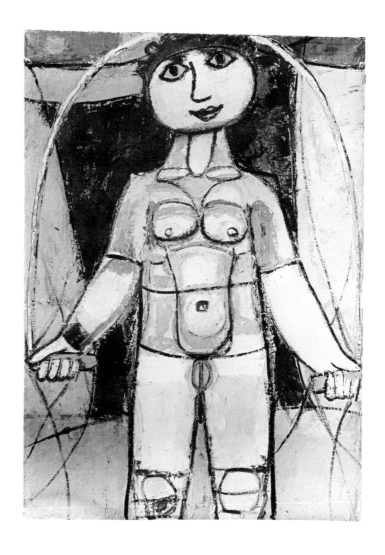

5

Métro, mars 1943
Metro, March 1943

Huile sur toile, 162 x 130 cm.
Oil on canvas, 63¾ x 51¼″

Private Collection

L. Fasc. I, fig. 31.

6

Vache et éleveur, septembre 1943
Cow and Breeder, September 1943

Huile sur toile, 92 x 73 cm.
Oil on canvas. 36¼ x 28¾ ″

Private Collection

L. Fasc. I, fig. 196.

7

Grande traite solitaire, octobre 1943
Great Solitary Milking, October 1943

Huile sur toile, 124 x 100 cm.
Oil on canvas, 48¾ x 39⅜″

Collection Charles Ratton, Paris

L. Fasc. I, fig. 198.

*8

Vue de Paris, la vie de plaisir,
février 1944
View of Paris, The Life of Pleasure,
February 1944

Huile sur toile, 88,5 x 116 cm.
Oil on canvas, 35 x 45¾″

Private Collection, New York

L. Fasc. I, fig. 224.

9

L'Accouchement, mars 1944
Childbirth, March 1944

Huile sur toile, 100 x 81 cm.
Oil on canvas, 39⅜ x 31⅞ ″

Private Collection

L. Fasc. I, fig. 233.

*10

Le Violoniste, mars 1944
Violinist, March 1944

Huile sur toile, 60 x 73 cm.
Oil on canvas, 23⅝ x 28¾″

Collection Mr. and Mrs. Gordon
Bunshaft, New York

L. Fasc. I, fig. 234.

11

Nature morte au jambon, mai 1944
Still Life with Ham, May 1944

Huile sur toile, 64,5 x 91,5 cm.
Oil on canvas, 25⅝ x 36″

Courtesy Sidney Janis Gallery,
New York

L. Fasc. I, fig. 243.

12

Paysage vineux, août 1944
Wine-Colored Landscape, August 1944

Huile sur toile, 125 x 95,5 cm.
Oil on canvas, 49¼ x 37⅝″

Collection André Malraux

L. Fasc. I, fig. 322.

Grand nu charbonneux, août 1944
Large Charcoal Nude, August 1944

Huile sur toile, 162 x 97 cm.
Oil on canvas, 63¾ x 38¼″

Lent by Galerie Beyeler, Basel

L. Fasc. I, fig. 326.

*14

Grand jazz band (Nouvelle Orléans),
décembre 1944
Grand Jazz Band (New Orleans),
December 1944

Huile sur toile, 114,5 x 147 cm.
Oil on canvas, 45⅛ x 57⅞″

Collection Mr. and Mrs. Gordon
Bunshaft, New York

L. Fasc. I, fig. 379.

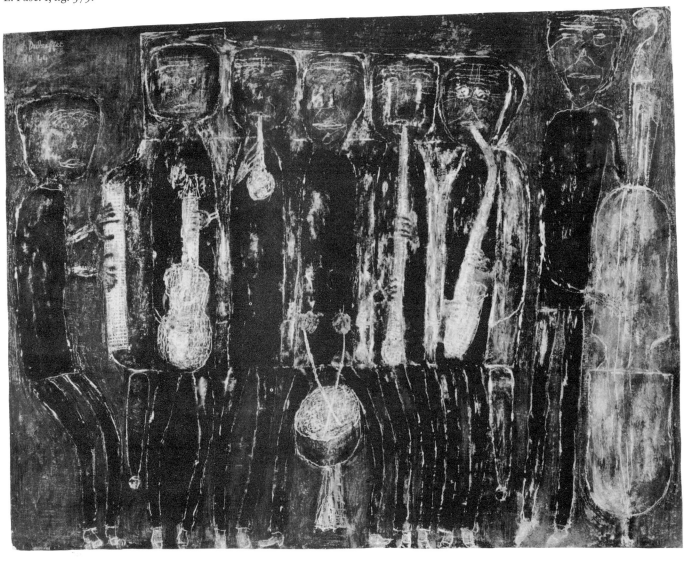

15

Fumeur au mur, avril 1945
Smoker by a Wall, April 1945

Huile sur toile, 116 x 89 cm.
Oil on canvas, 45¾ x 35″

Collection Julian J. Aberbach

L. Fasc. I, fig. 444.

16

Archétypes, mai 1945
Archetypes, May 1945

Haute pâte sur toile, 100 x 81 cm.
Thick impasto on canvas, 39⅜ x 31¾"

Collection particulière

L. Fasc. II, fig. 4.

*17

Femme incantant, juillet 1945
Incantatory Woman, July 1945

Haute pâte, 73 x 60 cm.
Swedish putty, 28¾ x 23⅝″

Anonymous Loan

L. Fasc. II, fig. 16.

*18

Gambadeuse d'asphalte,
novembre 1945
Asphalt Gamboller,
November 1945

Haute pâte sur toile, 92 x 65 cm.
Oil, gravel, stone on canvas, 36 x 25½"

Collection Mr. and Mrs. Jerome L.
Stern, New York

L. Fasc. II, fig. 85.

*19

Cafetière (ou Mouleuse de Café)
décembre 1945
Coffee Grinder, December 1945

Haute pâte sur toile, 116 x 89 cm.
Thick impasto on canvas, 45¾ x 35″

Collection Mr. and Mrs. Ralph F.
Colin, New York

L. Fasc. II, fig 93.

20

Volonté de puissance, janvier 1946
Will to Power, January 1946

Huile sur toile, 116 x 89 cm.
Oil on canvas, 45¾ x 35″

Collection particulière

L. Fasc. II, fig. 100.

21

Danseurs, février 1946
Dancing Partners, February 1946

Huile sur toile, 116 x 89 cm.
Oil on canvas, 45¾ x 35″

Collection particulière

L. Fasc. II, fig. 108.

22

Terracotta la grosse bouche,
février 1946
Terracotta Big Lips, February 1946

Huile sur toile, 100 x 81 cm.
Oil on canvas, 39⅜ x 31¾″

Collection Edward F. Dragon,
East Hampton, New York

L. Fasc. II, fig. 110.

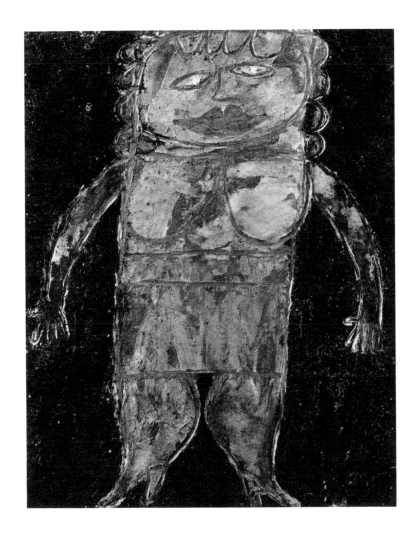

23

Touring Club, février 1946
Touring Club, February 1946

Haute pâte sur toile, 97 x 130 cm.
Thick impasto on canvas, 38 x 51″

Collection Richard S. Zeisler,
New York

L. Fasc. II, fig. 112.

Le Prince charmant, avril 1946
Prince Charming, April 1946

Haute pâte sur toile, 50 x 42,5 cm.
Thick impasto on canvas,
19¾ x 16¾″

Collection particulière

L. Fasc. II, fig. 133.

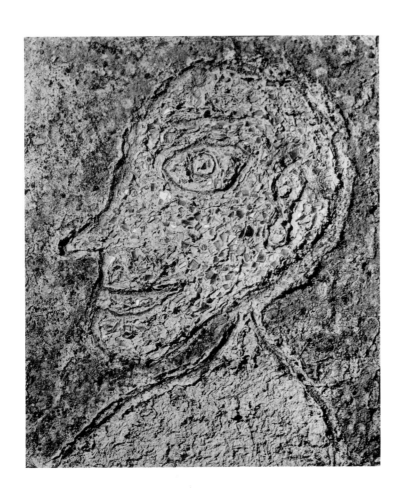

25

Michel Tapié soleil, août 1946
Michel Tapié, the Sun, August 1946

Matières diverses sur isorel,
109 x 87,5 cm.
Mixed media on masonite, 43 x 34½″

Private Collection

L. Fasc. III, fig. 35.

26

*Maast à crinière (Portrait de Jean
Paulhan)*, septembre 1946
*Maast with a Mane (Portrait of Jean
Paulhan)*, September 1946

Huile sur toile, 110 x 90 cm.
Oil on canvas, 43¼ x 35½″

Collection particulière

L. Fasc. III, fig. 45.

27

Tête de jeune fille aux cheveux blond cendré, septembre 1946
Head of a Girl with Ash Blond Hair, September 1946

Haute pâte sur isorel, 65 x 45 cm.
Thick impasto on masonite,
25½ x 17¾ ″

Collection Richard S. Zeisler,
New York

L. Fasc. III, fig. 52.

*28

Bertelé chat sauvage, décembre 1946
Bertelé Wildcat, December 1946

Huile sur toile (peinture emulsionnée),
130 x 97 cm.
Oil emulsion on canvas, 51 x 38″

Collection Miss Elizabeth Hahn,
New York

L. Fasc. III, fig. 97.

Antonin Artaud aux houppes,
janvier 1947
Antonin Artaud with Tassels,
January 1947

Huile sur toile (peinture emulsionnée),
130 x 97 cm.
Oil emulsion on canvas, 51 x 38″

Collection Mr. and Mrs.
Morton Neumann

L. Fasc. III, fig. 111.

30

Edith Boissonas Démon Thibétain,
février 1947
Edith Boissonas, Tibetan Demon,
February 1947

Huile et matières diverses sur toile,
130 x 97 cm.
Oil and mixed media on canvas,
51 x 38″

Lent by The Pace Gallery, New York

L. Fasc. III, fig. 123.

*31

Francis Ponge jubilation,
juillet-août 1947
Francis Ponge Jubilation,
July-August 1947

Chaux et plâtre sur isorel, 110 x 88 cm.
Whitewash and plaster on masonite,
43¼ x 34¾″

Courtesy Robert Elkon Gallery,
New York

L. Fasc. III, fig. 158.

32

Fautrier araignée au front,
juillet-août 1947
Fautrier with Spidered Brow,
July-August 1947

Huile sur toile (peinture emulsionnée),
116 x 89 cm.
Oil emulsion on canvas, 45¾ x 35″

Collection Robert Elkon, New York

L. Fasc. III, fig. 165.

Ils tiennent conseil, avril 1947
Holding Counsel, April 1947

Huile sur toile, 145 x 112 cm.
Oil on canvas, 57 x 44″

Collection Roger Goldet, Neuilly,
France

L. Fasc. IV, fig. 16.

34

Arabe et chameau bâté dans les dunes, 1948
Arab and Saddled Camel in the Dunes, 1948

Huile sur toile, 65 x 53 cm.
Oil on canvas, 25½ x 21″

Collection Edward F. Dragon,
East Hampton, New York

L. Fasc. IV, fig. 222.

35

L'Oiseleur, mai 1949
The Bird-Catcher, May 1949

Peinture à la colle sur toile de jute,
116 x 88,5 cm.
Distemper on burlap, 45¾ x 35″

Collection particulière

L. Fasc. V, fig. 47.

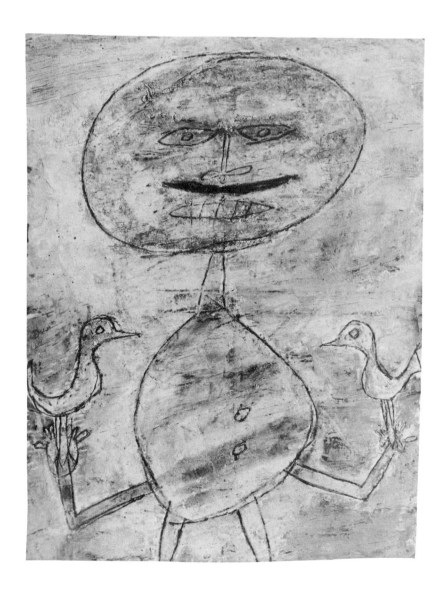

36

La Vie à la campagne, mai 1949
The Country Life, May 1949

Peinture à la colle sur toile,
116 x 89 cm.
Distemper on canvas, 45¾ x 35″

Private Collection

L. Fasc. V, fig. 48.

37

Le Chasseur, 21 mai 1949
The Hunter, May 21, 1949

Huile sur toile de jute, 89 x 116 cm.
Oil on burlap, 35 x 45¾″

Collection particulière

L. Fasc. V, fig. 52.

38

Dialogue aux oiseaux, 24 juin 1949
Dialogue in the Company of Birds,
June 24, 1949

Huile sur toile, 89 x 116 cm.
Oil on canvas, 35 x 45¾"

Private Collection

L. Fasc. V, fig. 72.

39

La Piste au désert, juillet 1949
The Desert Track, July 1949

Huile sur isorel, 50 x 61 cm.
Oil on masonite, 19¾ x 24″

Private Collection

L. Fasc. V, fig. 79.

40

Le Voyageur égaré,
21 ou 23 janvier 1950
The Strayed Traveler,
January 21 or 23, 1950

Huile sur toile (peinture emulsionnée),
130 x 195 cm.
Oil emulsion on canvas, 51 x 76¾"

Private Collection

L. Fasc. V, fig. 178.

41

L'Oursonne, avril 1950
Lady as a Bear Cub, April 1950

Huile sur toile, 116 x 89 cm.
Oil on canvas, 45¾ x 35″

Private Collection

L. Fasc. VI, fig. 83.

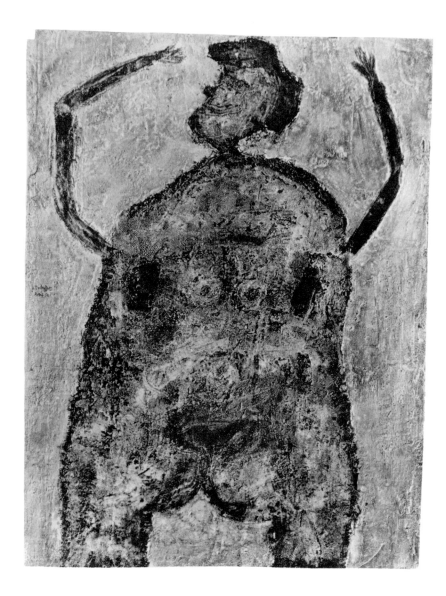

42

Olympia, avril 1950
Olympia, April 1950

Huile sur toile, 89 x 116 cm.
Oil on canvas, 35 x 45¾″

Collection Mrs. M. Victor Leventritt

L. Fasc. VI, fig. 85.

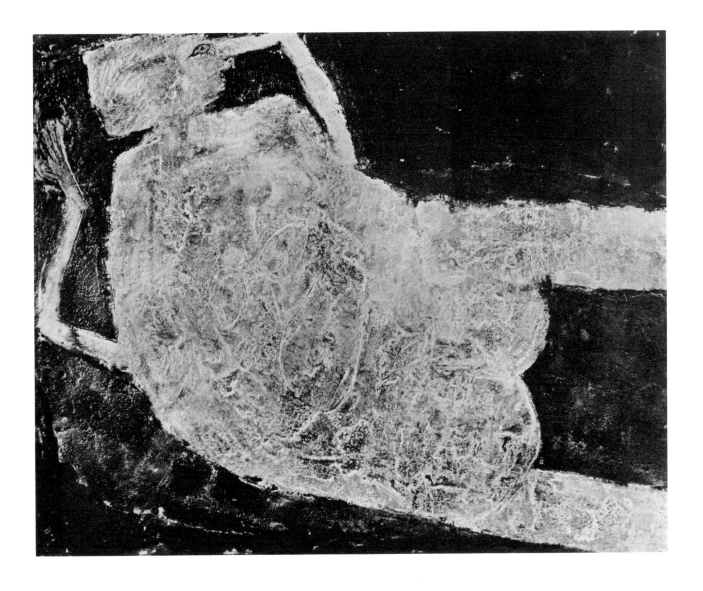

43

Corps de dame: gerbe bariolée,
août 1950
Gaudy Bunch of Flowers, August 1950

Huile sur toile, 116 x 89 cm.
Oil on canvas, 45¾ x 35″

Collection Mr. and Mrs. Martin A.
Fisher, New York

L. Fasc. VI, fig. 101.

44

Le Métafisyx, août 1950
Metaphysix, August 1950

Huile sur toile, 116 x 89 cm.
Oil on canvas, 45¾ x 35″

Collection particulière

L. Fasc. VI, fig. 102.

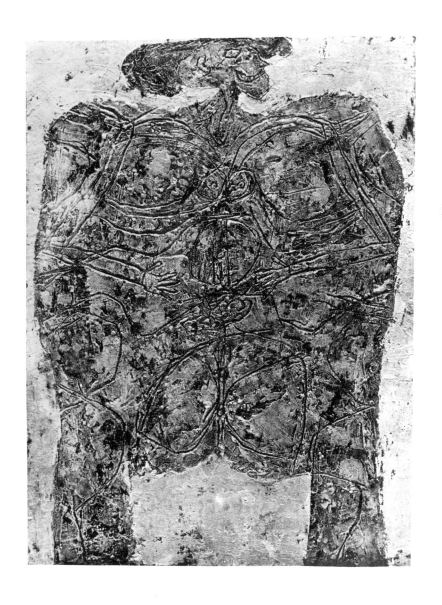

45

*Sang et feu (corps de dame aux chairs
rôties et rissolées)*, décembre 1950
*Blood and Fire (Corps de Dame with
Roasted and Browned Flesh)*,
December 1950

Huile sur toile, 116 x 89 cm.
Oil on canvas, 45¾ x 35″

Private Collection, New York

L. Fasc. VI, fig. 113.

Triomphe et gloire, décembre 1950
Triumph and Glory, December 1950

Huile sur toile, 130 x 97 cm.
Oil on canvas, 51 x 38″

Collection The Solomon R.
Guggenheim Museum, New York

L. Fasc. VI, fig. 115.

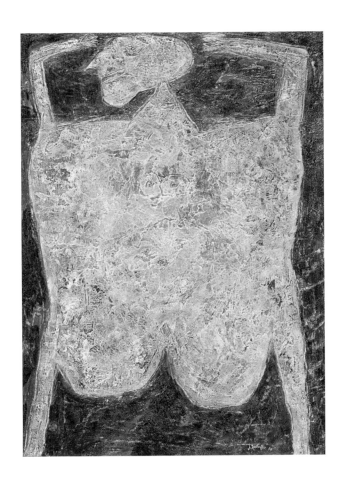

47

Concentration fluidique, 4 février 1951
Concentration of Fluids,
February 4, 1951

Huile sur toile, 116 x 89 cm.
Oil on canvas, 45¾ x 35″

Collection Alfonso A. Ossorio,
East Hampton, New York

L. Fasc. VI, fig. 117.

48

Le Géologue, décembre 1950
The Geologist, December 1950

Huile sur toile, 97 x 130 cm.
Oil on canvas, 38 x 51″

Private Collection

L. Fasc. VII, fig. 1.

49

Table aux pièces d'histoire naturelle,
février 1951
*Table Covered with Natural History
Specimens,* February 1951

Huile sur toile, 146 x 114 cm.
Oil on canvas, 57½ x 44⅞″

Collection Mr. and Mrs. Ralph F.
Colin, New York

L. Fasc. VII, fig. 12.

50

Table au flacon cravaté, 8-15 août 1951
*Table with a Bottle Wearing a
Necktie,* August 8-15, 1951

Huile sur isorel, 65 x 81 cm.
Oil on masonite, 25½ x 32″

Private Collection

L. Fasc. VII, fig. 62.

51

Le Mage au nez fin, janvier 1952
The Fine-Nosed Magus, January 1952

Huile sur toile, 61 x 51 cm.
Oil on canvas, 24 x 20″

Collection particulière

L. Fasc. VII, fig. 133.

52

Les Roses de la terre, février 1952
Roses of the Earth, February 1952

Huile sur toile, 115 x 152 cm.
Oil on canvas, 45¼ x 59⅞″

Private Collection

L. Fasc. VII, fig. 185.

53

Peuplements au sol, février 1952
Throngs of the Earth, February 1952

Huile sur isorel, 66 x 81 cm.
Oil on masonite, 26 x 32″

Collection Musée des Arts Décoratifs,
Paris/Donation Jean Dubuffet

L. Fasc. VII, fig. 186.

54

Pierre de Dordogne, juin 1952
Stone of Dordogne, June 1952

Huile sur isorel, 91 x 122 cm.
Oil on masonite, 35⅞ x 48″

Private Collection

L. Fasc. VII, fig. 206.

55

Pierre aux figures, juillet 1952
Stone with Figures, July 1952

Huile sur isorel, 89 x 116 cm.
Oil on masonite, 35 x 45¾″

Collection particulière

L. Fasc. VII, fig. 214.

56

Le Voyageur sans boussole,
8 juillet 1952
Traveler without a Compass,
July 8, 1952

Huile sur isorel, 118 x 155 cm.
Oil on masonite, 46½ x 61″

Collection particulière

L. Fasc. VII, fig. 217.

57

Extase au ciel, juillet 1952
Ecstasy in the Sky, July 1952

Huile sur isorel, 115 x 88 cm.
Oil on masonite, 45¼ x 34¾ ″

Private Collection

L. Fasc. VII, fig. 220.

58

Le Pays hanté, 15-16 août 1952
Haunted Country, August 15-16, 1952

Huile sur isorel, 65 x 81 cm.
Oil on masonite, 25½ x 32″

Private Collection

L. Fasc. VII, fig. 227.

59

La Butte aux visions, 23 août 1952
Knoll of Visions, August 23, 1952

Huile sur isorel, 150 x 195 cm.
Oil on masonite, 59 x 76¾″

Collection particulière

L. Fasc. VII, fig. 235.

60

Le Montreur d'agate, novembre 1952
Man Displaying an Agate,
November 1952

Huile sur toile, 81 x 65 cm.
Oil on canvas, 32 x 25½".

Private Collection

L. Fasc. VIII, fig. 14.

61

Paysage métapsychique,
décembre 1952
Metapsychical Landscape,
December 1952

Huile, colle, matières diverses sur
toile, 130 x 162 cm.
Oil, glue, mixed media on canvas,
51 x 63¾″

Collection Mr. and Mrs. Richard L.
Feigen, Bedford, New York

L. Fasc. VIII, fig. 23.

62

La Chèvre égarée, 18-19 janvier 1953
The Stray Goat, January 18-19, 1953

Huile sur toile, 89 x 116 cm.
Oil on canvas, 35 x 45¾″

Private Collection

L. Fasc. VIII, fig. 33.

63

Flacon, lettres, ciseaux, juin 1953
Bottle, Letters, Scissors, June 1953

Huile sur toile, 81 x 100 cm.
Oil on canvas, 32 x 39⅜″

Collection Max Loreau, Belgium

L. Fasc. VIII, fig. 79.

64

La Vie affairée, août 1953
The Busy Life, August 1953

Huile sur toile, 130 x 195 cm.
Oil on canvas, 51 x 76¾″

Collection The Tate Gallery, London

L. Fasc. VIII, fig. 89.

65

Cheveux de Sylvain,
ca. septembre 1953
Sylvan Hair, ca. September 1953

Ailes de papillons sylvains,
26,5 x 17,5 cm.
White admiral butterfly wings,
10½ x 6⅞″

Collection Franz Meyer, Basel

L. Fasc. IX, fig. 1.

66

L'Age a écrit sur leurs visages,
janvier-février 1954
Age has Written on their Faces,
January-February 1954

Huile sur toile, 91 x 72 cm.
Oil on canvas, 35⅞ x 28¼″

Collection particulière

L. Fasc. IX, fig. 127.

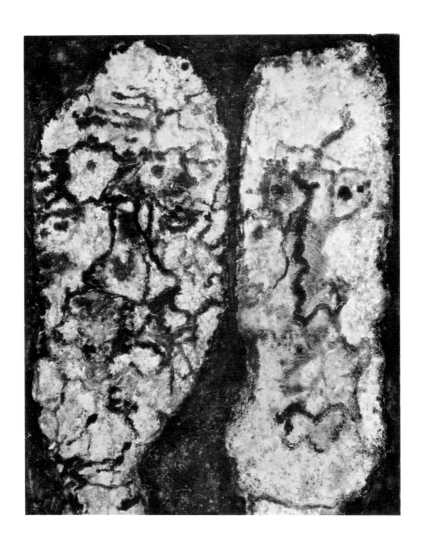

*67

Le Dépénaillé, avril 1954
The Ragged One, April 1954

Mâchefer, h. 71 cm.
Clinker, 28″ h.

Collection Mr. and Mrs. Gordon
Bunshaft, New York

L. Fasc. X, fig. 7.

*68

Le Magicien, septembre 1954
The Magician, September 1954

Scories et racines, h. 110 cm.
Slag and roots, 43¼″ h.

Collection The Museum of Modern
Art, New York, Gift of Mr. and
Mrs. N. Richard Miller and Mr. and
Mrs. Alex L. Hillman and Samuel
Girard Funds, 1968

L. Fasc. X, fig. 38.

69

Le Morvandiau, octobre 1954
Man from Morvan, October 1954

Charbon de bois, h. 62 cm.
Charcoal, 24½″ h.

Collection particulière

L. Fasc. X, fig. 43.

L'Extravagante, juillet 1954
Extravagant Lady, July 1954

Huile sur toile, 92 x 73 cm.
Oil on canvas, 36 x 28¾"

Private Collection

L. Fasc. X, fig. 67.

Vache à l'herbage, août 1954
Cow in Pasture, August 1954

Huile sur toile, 96 x 114 cm.
Oil on canvas, 37¾ x 44⅞"

Collection Mr. and Mrs. Ralph F.
Colin, New York

L. Fasc. X, fig. 105.

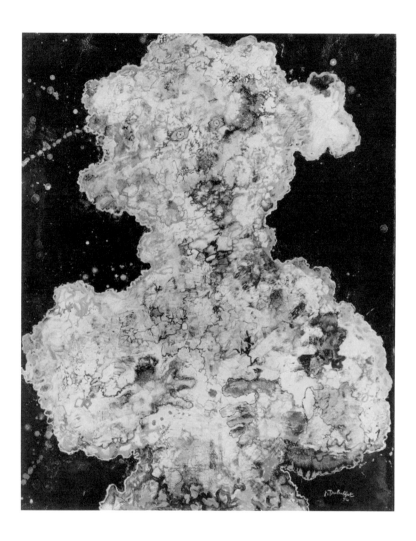

*72

Vache tachetée, août 1954
Spotted Cow, August 1954

Huile sur toile, 89 x 117 cm.
Oil on canvas, 35 x 46"

Collection Mr. and Mrs. Gordon
Bunshaft, New York

L. Fasc. X, fig. 106.

73

Vache au pré noir, octobre 1954
Cow in a Black Meadow,
October 1954

Huile sur toile, 146 x 114 cm.
Oil on canvas, 57½ x 44⅞″

Collection particulière

L. Fasc. X, fig. 110.

*74

Vache la Belle Allègre, décembre 1954
Cow, The Merry Beauty,
December 1954

Huile sur toile, 116 x 89 cm.
Oil on canvas, 45¾ x 35″

Private Collection, London

L. Fasc. X, fig. 117.

75

Mon char, mon jardin, juin 1955
My Cart, My Garden, June 1955

Huile sur toile, 89 x 116 cm.
Oil on canvas, 35 x 45¾″

Collection James Thrall Soby

L. Fasc. XI, fig. 69.

76

Le Chien rôdeur, août 1955
Prowling Dog, August 1955

Huile sur toile, 81 x 100 cm.
Oil on canvas, 32 x 39⅜"

Collection Mr. and Mrs. Arthur J.
Kobacker, Steubenville, Ohio

L. Fasc. XI, fig. 76.

*77

Barbu oreillu, juillet 1955
Bearded Man with Large Ears,
July 1955

Ailes de papillons, 33 x 23 cm.
Butterfly wings, 13 x 9″

Collection Mr. and Mrs. Morton L.
Janklow, New York

L. Fasc. XI, fig. 124.

78

Portrait de Jean Paulhan, juillet 1955
Portrait of Jean Paulhan, July 1955

Ailes de papillons, 45,5 x 30,5 cm.
Butterfly wings, 17⅞ x 12″

Collection particulière, Paris

L. Fasc. XI, fig. 127.

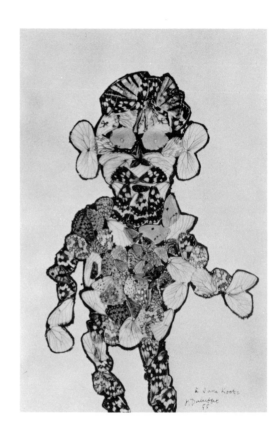

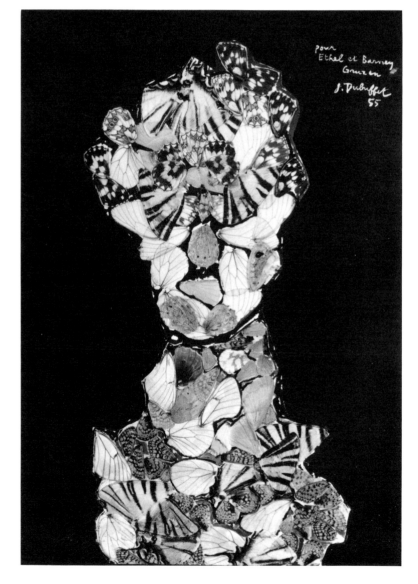

79

Jardin d'or et noir, août 1955
Black and Gold Garden, August 1955

Ailes de papillons, 22 x 27 cm.
Butterfly wings, 8⅝ x 10⅝″

Collection particulière

L. Fasc. XI, fig. 132.

80

Jardin de Bibi Trompette, août 1955
The Garden of Bibi Trompette,
August 1955

Ailes de papillons, 23 x 32 cm.
Butterfly wings, 9 x 12½″

Collection Pomona College, Clare-
mont, California, Gift of Norton
Simon, 1957

L. Fasc. XI, fig. 138.

81

La Quémandeuse, 3 septembre 1955
The Beggar, September 3, 1955

Huile sur toile, 92 x 73 cm.
Oil on canvas, 36 x 28¾″

Private Collection

L. Fasc. XI, fig. 158

82

Le Petit jardinier, octobre 1955
The Little Gardener, October 1955

Huile sur toile, 73 x 92 cm.
Oil on canvas, 28¾ x 36″

Collection Edwin Janss, Jr., Thousand
Oaks, California

L. Fasc. XI, fig. 180.

83

Jardin de Fouille-Roucoule,
novembre 1955
The Garden of Fouille-Roucoule,
November 1955

Huile sur toile (assemblage),
116 x 89 cm.
Oil on canvas (assemblage), 45¾ x 35″

Collection particulière

L. Fasc. XII, fig. 3.

84

Les Jardins de la chaussée,
25 janvier 1956
The Gardens of the Highway,
January 25, 1956

Huile sur toile (assemblage),
125 x 99 cm.
Oil on canvas (assemblage), 49¼ x 39″

Private Collection

L. Fasc. XII, fig. 22.

85

Court l'herbe, sautent cailloux,
juin 1956
Run Grass, Jump Pebbles, June 1956

Huile sur toile (assemblage),
201 x 154 cm.
Oil on canvas (assemblage),
79½ x 60⅝″

Collection particulière

L. Fasc. XII, fig. 52.

86

La Pointe au pitre, septembre 1956
Clown's Point, September 1956

Huile sur toile (assemblage),
144 x 116 cm.
Oil on canvas (assemblage),
56¾ x 45¾″

Private Collection

L. Fasc. XII, fig. 68.

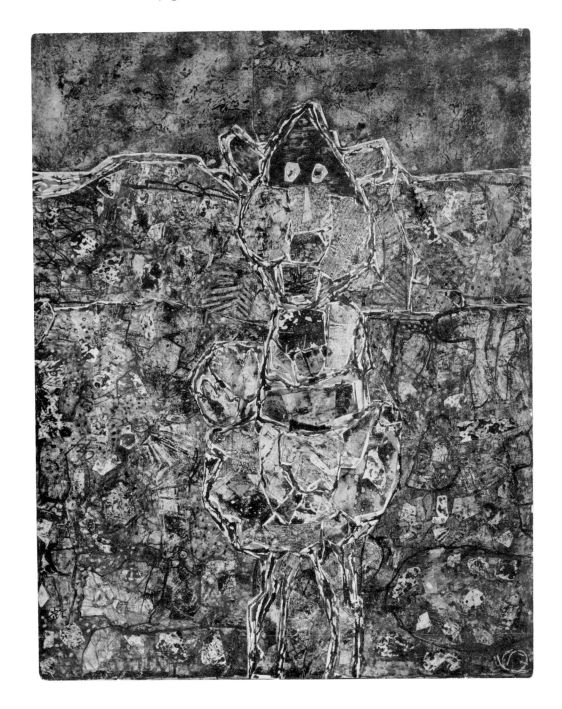

87

Table au tiroir, novembre 1956
Table with Drawer, November 1956

Huile sur toile, 89 x 116 cm.
Oil on canvas, 35 x 45¾"

Collection Stedelijk Museum,
Amsterdam

L. Fasc. XII, fig. 86.

88

Chalumo dardar, décembre 1956
Chalumo dardar, December 1956

Huile sur toile (assemblage),
81 x 51 cm.
Oil on canvas (assemblage), 32 x 20″

Collection particulière

L. Fasc. XII, fig. 98.

89

Lecture au sol, 18 juillet 1957
Reading of the Soil, July 18, 1957

Huile sur toile (assemblage),
141 x 183 cm.
Oil on canvas (assemblage), 55½ x 72″

Collection particulière

L. Fasc. XIII, fig. 63.

90

Porte au chiendent, 31 octobre 1957
Door with Couchgrass,
October 31, 1957

Huile sur toile, 189 x 146 cm.
Oil on canvas, 74½ x 57½″

Collection The Solomon R.
Guggenheim Museum, New York

L. Fasc. XIII, fig. 102.

91

Texturologie VII (ombreuse et rousse),
29-30 novembre 1957 (daté décembre)
Texturology VII (Reddened Shadows),
November 29-30, 1957 (dated
December)

Huile sur toile, 130 x 162 cm.
Oil on canvas, 51¼ x 63¾"

Collection Musée des Arts Décoratifs,
Paris/Donation Jean Dubuffet

L. Fasc. XIII, fig. 130.

92

Table (de sérénité), 5 décembre 1957
Table (of Serenity), December 5, 1957

Huile sur toile, 114 x 146 cm.
Oil on canvas, 44⅞ x 57½"

Collection Max Loreau, Belgium

L. Fasc. XIII, fig. 136.

93

Vieille peau de l'esplanade (Texturo-logie XXXI), 13 avril 1958
Aged Skin of the Esplanade (Texturology XXXI), April 13, 1958

Huile sur toile, 114 x 146 cm.
Oil on canvas, 44⅞ x 57½″

Collection The St. Louis Art Museum, Gift of Mr. and Mrs. Joseph Pulitzer, Jr.

L. Fasc. XIII, fig. 200.

94

Hauts lieux du mariage (Portraits de Werner et Nora Schenk),
7 juin-octobre 1958
The Heights of Marriage (Portraits of Werner and Nora Schenk),
June 7-October 1958

Huile sur toile, 92 x 73 cm.
Oil on canvas, 36 x 28¾″

Private Collection

L. Fasc. XIV, fig. 18.

95

Pullulation (Texturologie XLII),
27 mai 1958
Pullulation (Texturology XLII),
May 27, 1958

Huile sur toile, 89 x 116 cm.
Oil on canvas, 35 x 45¾″

Collection Mr. and Mrs. Morton L.
Janklow, New York

L. Fasc. XIV, fig. 31.

96

*Vie exemplaire du sol (Texturologie
LXIII),* 13 octobre 1958
*The Exemplary Life of the Soil
(Texturology LXIII),* October 13, 1958

Huile sur toile, 130 x 162 cm.
Oil on canvas, 51 x 63¾″

Collection The Tate Gallery, London

L. Fasc. XIV, fig. 59.

97

Topographie honneur du sol, début
décembre 1958
Topography Honor of the Soil, early
December 1958

Huile sur toile (assemblage),
90 x 154 cm.
Oil on canvas (assemblage),
35½ x 60¾ "

Collection particulière

L. Fasc. XIV, fig. 90.

98

Barbe de lumière des aveuglés,
juillet 1959
Beard of Blinding Light, July 1959

Huile sur toile (assemblage),
116 x 74 cm.
Oil on canvas (assemblage),
45¾ x 29¼ "

Collection particulière

L. Fasc. XV, fig. 54.

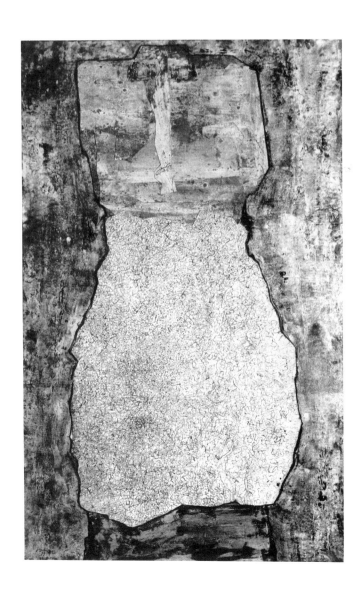

99

Table de barbe, octobre 1959
Beard Table, October 1959

Huile sur toile, 130 x 97 cm.
Oil on canvas, 51 x 38″

Collection particulière

L. Fasc. XV, fig. 77.

Déclinaison de barbe, novembre 1959
Beard Declension, November 1959

Huile sur toile, 130 x 97 cm.
Oil on canvas, 51 x 38″

Collection particulière

L. Fasc. XV, fig. 83.

*101

Tabac barbiche, août 1959
Tobacco Man with Goatee,
August 1959

Eléments botaniques (Scolopendre,
Platane), 51 x 33 cm.
Botanical elements (Hart's Tongue,
Plane-tree), 20 x 13″

Collection Mr. and Mrs. Morton L.
Janklow, New York

L. Fasc. XVII, fig. 14.

102

Collet monté, décembre 1959
Stiff Shirt, December 1959

Eléments botaniques, 65 x 43 cm.
Botanical elements, 25½ x 17″

Collection Alphonse Chave

L. Fasc. XVII, fig. 48.

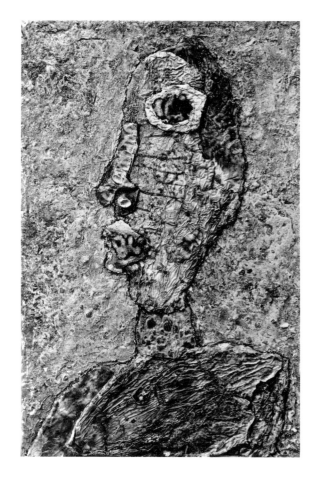

103

La Mer de peau, décembre 1959
Sea of Skin, December 1959

Eléments botaniques (Agave bleue),
55 x 46 cm.
Botanical elements (Blue Agave),
21⅝ x 18″

Collection particulière

L. Fasc. XVII, fig. 53.

104

Chaussée boiseuse, décembre 1959
Wooded Causeway, December 1959

Eléments botaniques, 46 x 55 cm.
Botanical elements, 18 x 21⅝″

Collection particulière

L. Fasc. XVII, fig. 54.

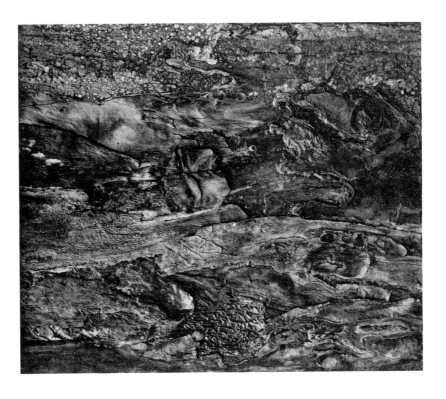

105

L'Inconsistant, septembre 1959
The Insubstantial One, September 1959

Huile sur toile, 116 x 89 cm.
Oil on canvas, 45¾ x 35″

Collection particulière

L. Fasc. XVII, fig. 57.

106

L'Aveugle, octobre 1959
Blind Man, October 1959

Papier d'argent, h. 33 cm.
Metal foil, 13″ h.

Collection Mr. and Mrs. Ralph F. Colin, New York

L. Fasc. XVII, fig. 63.

107

Grise mine, octobre 1959
Icy Mien, October 1959

Bois de la plage, h. 42 cm.
Driftwood, 16½″ h.

Collection M. et Mme. Daniel
Varenne, Paris

L. Fasc. XVII, fig. 65.

108

Le Vieux de la plage, novembre 1959
The Old Man of the Beach,
November 1959

Bois de la plage, h. 34 cm.
Driftwood, 13⅜″ h.

Collection M. et Mme. Daniel
Varenne, Paris

L. Fasc. XVII, fig. 71.

*109

Minaudage aux dents, 4 décembre 1959
Toothy Smirk, December 4, 1959

Papier mâché, h. 37 cm.
Papier mâché, 14½″ h.

Collection Mr. and Mrs. Morton L.
Janklow, New York

L. Fasc. XVII, fig. 82.

110

Pince-bec, 23 juin-août 1960
Pinched Lips, June 23-August 1960

Papier mâché, h. 95 cm.
Papier mâché, 37⅜" h.

Collection Jean Dubuffet

L. Fasc. XVII, fig. 121.

111

Substance d'astre, décembre 1959
The Substance of Stars, December 1959

Papier d'argent, 150 x 195 cm.
Metal foil, 59 x 76¾˝

Collection particulière

L. Fasc. XVII, fig. 91.

112

Messe de terre, décembre 1959-
mai 1960
Rite of the Earth, December 1959-
May 1960

Papier mâché, 150 x 195 cm.
Papier mâché, 59 x 76¾ ″

Collection particulière

L. Fasc. XVII, fig. 101.

113

Terre mère, décembre 1959-mai 1960
Mother Earth, December 1959-
May 1960

Pâte plastique, 153 x 200 cm.
Plastic paste, 60¼ x 78¾"

Collection particulière

L. Fasc. XVII, fig. 102.

114

Fruits de terre, décembre 1960
Fruits of the Earth, December 1960

Papier mâché et pâte vinylique,
81 x 100 cm.
Papier mâché and vinyl paste,
32 x 39⅜"

Collection Musée des Arts Décoratifs,
Paris/Donation Jean Dubuffet

L. Fasc. XVII, fig. 150.

115

L'Or, décembre 1959-62
Gold, December 1959-62

Papier doré sur isorel, 76 x 105 cm.
Gold foil on masonite, 30 x 41⅜"

Collection Mrs. Vera Nathhorst,
Stockholm

L. Fasc. XVII, fig. 151.

116

Paris-Montparnasse, 5-21 mars 1961
Paris-Montparnasse, March 5-21, 1961

Huile sur toile, 165 x 220 cm.
Oil on canvas, 65 x 86½"

Collection particulière

L. Fasc. XIX, fig. 20.

*117

Les Grandes artères, 3-8 juillet 1961
Major Thoroughfares, July 3-8, 1961

Huile sur toile, 114 x 146 cm.
Oil on canvas, 44⅞ x 57½"

Collection Mr. and Mrs. Myron A.
Minskoff, New York

L. Fasc. XIX, fig. 94.

118

La Gigue irlandaise,
18-19 septembre 1961
Irish Jig, September 18-19, 1961

Huile sur toile, 114 x 146 cm.
Oil on canvas, 44⅞ x 57½″

Collection particulière

L. Fasc. XIX, fig. 162.

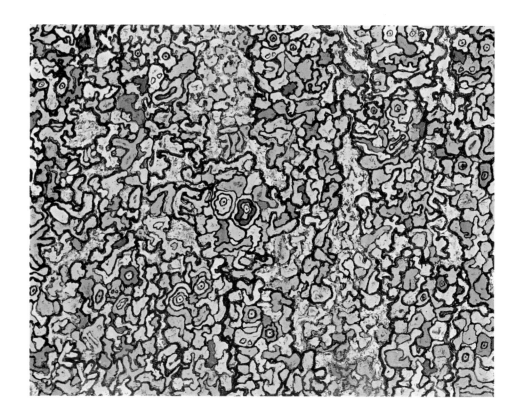

Le Plomb dans l'aile,
1-3 novembre 1961
Hard Hit, November 1-3, 1961

Huile sur toile, 190 x 250 cm.
Oil on canvas, 74⅞ x 98½"

Collection The Detroit Institute of
Arts, Gift of W. Hawkins Ferry

L. Fasc. XIX, fig. 212.

120

L'Instant propice, 2-3 janvier 1962
Propitious Moment, January 2-3, 1962

Huile sur toile, 200 x 165 cm.
Oil on canvas, 78¾ x 65″

Collection particulière

L. Fasc. XIX, fig. 265.

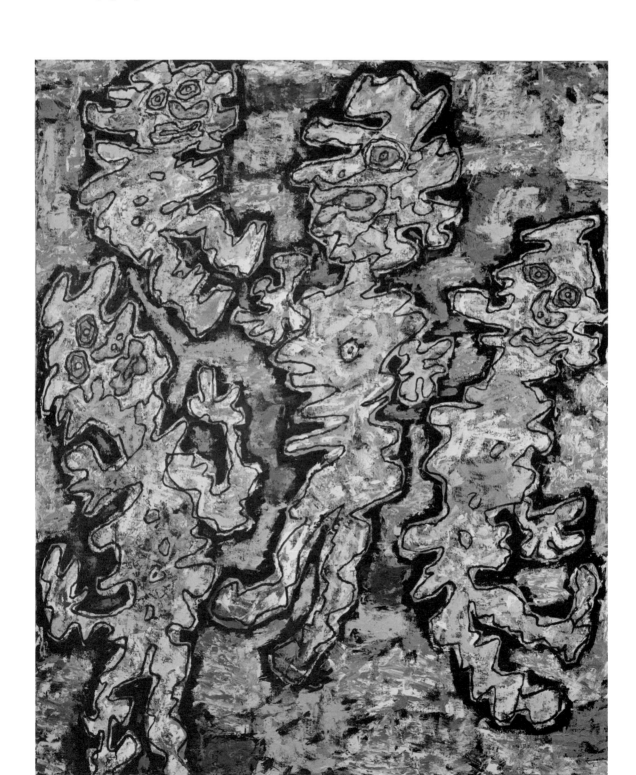

121

Rue de l'Entourloupe, 24 février 1963
Rue de l'Entourloupe,
February 24, 1963

Huile sur toile, 89 x 116 cm.
Oil on canvas, 35 x 45¾"

Lent by The Pace Gallery, New York

L. Fasc. XX, fig. 125.

122

Les Riches fruits de l'erreur,
12 mars 1963
The Rich Fruits of Error,
March 12, 1963

Huile sur toile, 114 x 146 cm.
Oil on canvas, 44⅞ x 57½″

Collection Max Loreau, Belgium

L. Fasc. XX, fig. 129.

123

Etre et paraître, 25 juillet 1963
Being and Appearing, July 25, 1963

Huile sur toile, 150 x 195 cm.
Oil on canvas, 59 x 76¾″

Collection particulière

L. Fasc. XX, fig. 158.

124

La Marée l'Hourloupe,
11-23 octobre 1963
The Tide of the Hourloupe,
October 11-23, 1963

Huile sur toile, 220 x 300 cm.
Oil on canvas, 86½ x 118¼″

Collection particulière

L. Fasc. XX, fig. 182.

125

Le Cosmopolite, 8 décembre 1963
The Cosmopolitan, December 8, 1963

Huile sur toile, 195 x 130 cm.
Oil on canvas, 76¾ x 51″

Collection The Stedelijk Museum,
Amsterdam

L. Fasc. XX, fig. 230.

126

Trotte la houle, 9 juillet 1964
Ride the Wave, July 9, 1964

Huile sur toile, 89 x 116 cm.
Oil on canvas, 35 x 45¾"

Collection particulière

L. Fasc. XX, fig. 368.

127

La Brouette II, 17 juillet 1964
Wheelbarrow II, July 17, 1964

Huile sur toile, 89 x 116 cm.
Oil on canvas, 35 x 45¾″

Collection particulière

L. Fasc. XX, fig. 374.

128

Délibération du lavabo (Lavabo V),
21 mars 1965
*Deliberation on a Washbasin
(Washbasin V)*, March 21, 1965

Vinyle sur toile, 130 x 162 cm.
Vinyl on canvas, 51 x 63¾″

Collection particulière

L. Fasc. XXI, fig. 87.

129

Presque midi (Pendule I), 20 avril 1965
Almost Noon (Clock I), April 20, 1965

Vinyle sur toile, 130 x 97 cm.
Vinyl on canvas, 51 x 38¼″

Collection particulière

L. Fasc. XXI, fig. 120.

130

Le Train de pendules, 24-28 avril 1965
Train of Clocks, April 24-28, 1965

Vinyle sur papier entoilé; 2 panneaux
de 125 x 200 cm. chaque
Vinyl on paper on canvas; 2 sections,
each 49¼ x 78¾"

Collections Nationales, Paris

L. Fasc. XXI, fig. 122.

131

Illustration du robinet (Robinet IV),
29-30 avril 1965
Illustration of a Faucet (Faucet IV),
April 29-30, 1965

Vinyle sur toile, 162 x 130 cm.
Vinyl on canvas, 63⅞ x 51″

Private Collection

L. Fasc. XXI, fig. 123.

132

Nunc Stans, 16 mai-5 juin 1965
Nunc Stans, May 16-June 5, 1965

Vinyle sur toile; 3 panneaux de
161,9 x 274 cm. chaque
Vinyl on canvas; 3 sections, each
63¾ x 107⅞"

Collection The Solomon R.
Guggenheim Museum, New York

L. Fasc. XXI, fig. 143.

133

Cafetière I, 14 décembre 1965
Coffee Pot I, December 14, 1965

Vinyle sur papier entoilé, 105 x 70 cm.
Vinyl on paper on canvas,
41⅜ x 27½″

Collection Max Loreau, Belgium

L. Fasc. XXI, fig. 190.

134

Fusil canardier, 30 janvier 1966
Duck-Shooting Gun, January 30, 1966

Vinyle sur toile, 125 x 200 cm.
Vinyl on canvas, 49¼ x 78¾″

Collection Mr. and Mrs. Charles M.
Diker

L. Fasc. XXI, fig. 218.

*135

Cuisinière à gaz I, 23 février 1966
Gas Stove I, February 23, 1966

Vinyle sur toile, 130 x 97 cm.
Vinyl on canvas, 51¼ x 42″

Collection Arnold and Milly Glimcher,
New York

L. Fasc. XXI, fig. 256

Demeure V (aux escaliers et nombreuses chambres) 8 avril 1966
Dwelling V (with Stairways and Many Rooms) April 8, 1966

Vinyle sur toile, 146 x 114 cm.
Vinyl on canvas, 57½ x 44⅞"

Collection Mr. and Mrs. Gordon Bunshaft, New York

L. Fasc. XXI, fig. 339.

137

Offres galantes, 27 janvier 1967
Gallant Offers, January 27, 1967

Vinyle sur toile, 130 x 162 cm.
Vinyl on canvas, 51 x 63⅞″

Collection particulière

L. Fasc. XXII, fig. 299.

138

Ciseaux IV (fond bleu),
18 février 1967
Scissors IV (Blue Ground),
February 18, 1967

Vinyle sur toile, 146 x 114 cm.
Vinyl on canvas, 57½ x 44⅞"

Collection particulière

L. Fasc. XXII, fig. 332.

139

Escalier funéraire pour Jacques
Ulmann (Escalier IX), 2 mai 1967
Funerary Staircase for Jacques Ulmann
(Staircase IX), May 2, 1967

Vinyle sur toile, 272 x 163 cm.
Vinyl on canvas, 107¼ x 64¼″

Collection Museum Boymans van-
Beuningen, Rotterdam

L. Fasc. XXII, fig. 410.

140

Vieil homme à la canne, 5 mai 1967
Old Man with a Cane, May 5, 1967

Vinyle sur toile, 130 x 97 cm.
Vinyl on canvas, 51 x 38″

Collection particulière

L. Fasc. XXII, fig. 411.

141

Métro (Recueil de 12 gouaches et couverture), mars 1943
Metro (Album of 12 gouaches and cover design), March 1943

Gouache, 37 x 30 cm.
Gouache, 14½ x 11⅞"

Section II Works on paper including prints

II Oeuvres sur papier, y compris les oeuvres graphiques

a. *Couverture du livre sur le métro*
Cover for book on the Metro

Private Collection

L. Fasc. I, fig. 32.

b. *Métro*
   Private Collection
   L. Fasc. I, fig. 33.

c. *Métro*
   Private Collection
   L. Fasc. I, fig. 34.

d. *Métro*
   Private Collection
   L. Fasc. I, fig. 35.

e. *Métro*
   Private Collection
   L. Fasc. I, fig. 36.

f. *Métro*
    Private Collection
    L. Fasc. I, fig. 37.

g. *Métro*
    Private Collection
    L. Fasc. I, fig. 38.

h. *Métro*
    Private Collection
    L. Fasc. I, fig. 39.

i. *Métro*
    Private Collection
    L. Fasc. I, fig. 40.

j. *Métro*
Private Collection
L. Fasc. I, fig. 41.

k. *Métro*
Private Collection
L. Fasc. I, fig. 42.

l. *Métro*
Private Collection
L. Fasc. I, fig. 43.

m. *Métro*
Collection M. et Mme. Daniel
Varenne, Paris
L. Fasc. I, fig. 44.

142
Vue de Paris (place de l'Estrapade),
avril 1943
View of Paris (place de l'Estrapade),
April 1943

Gouache, 30 x 37 cm.
Gouache, 11⅞ x 14½"

Lent by The Pace Gallery, New York

L. Fasc. I, fig. 50.

Cycliste, ca. septembre 1944
Cyclist, ca. September 1944

Gouache, 25 x 15 cm.
Gouache, 9⅞ x 5⅞″

Collection Mr. and Mrs. N.
Richard Miller

Campagne aux cyclistes, juillet 1943
Landscape with Cyclists, July 1943

Gouache, 25 x 15 cm.
Gouache, 9⅞ x 5⅞″

Collection Musée des Arts Décoratifs,
Paris/Donation Jean Dubuffet

L. Fasc. I, fig. 76.

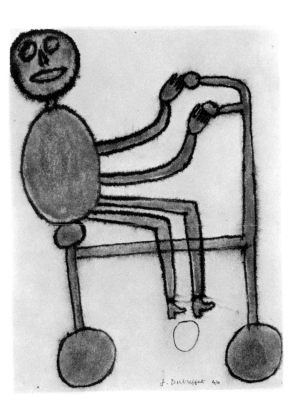

145

Trois hommes dans la forêt,
20 mai 1944
Three Men in the Forest, May 20, 1944

Encre de Chine, 25,5 x 16,5 cm.
India ink, 10 x 6½″

Private Collection

L. Fasc. I, fig. 249.

146

Message: "Dubuffet est un sale
con . . .", 24 juin 1944
Message, June 24, 1944

Encre de Chine, 25,5 x 25,5 cm.
India ink, 10 x 10″

Collection Alfonso A. Ossorio,
East Hampton, New York

L. Fasc. I, fig. 278.

147

Message: ". . . ma santé toujours
excellente", 24 juin 1944
Message, June 24, 1944

Encre de Chine, 20,5 x 26 cm.
India ink, 8⅛ x 10¼″

Collection Edward F. Dragon,
East Hampton, New York

L. Fasc. I, fig. 279.

148

La Plage à Cassis, juin 1944
The Beach at Cassis, June 1944

Encre de Chine, 33 x 25 cm.
India ink, 13 x 9⅜″

Collection Mr. and Mrs. Richard L.
Feigen, Bedford, New York

L. Fasc. I, fig. 309.

149

Femme assise au fauteuil, juillet 1944
Woman in an Armchair, July 1944

Gouache, 26 x 19 cm.
Gouache, 10¼ x 7½"

Collection M. et Mme. Daniel
Varenne, Paris

L. Fasc. I, fig. 305.

150

Cycliste nue, 28 juillet 1944
Nude Cyclist, July 28, 1944

Gouache, 31 x 23 cm.
Gouache, 12¼ x 9″

Collection M. et Mme. Daniel
Varenne, Paris

L. Fasc. I, fig. 316.

151

Homme léchant l'oeillet,
septembre 1945
Man Licking a Carnation,
September 1945

Gouache, 27 x 22 cm.
Gouache, 10¾ x 8¾″

Lent by Galerie Beyeler, Basel

L. Fasc. II, fig. 52.

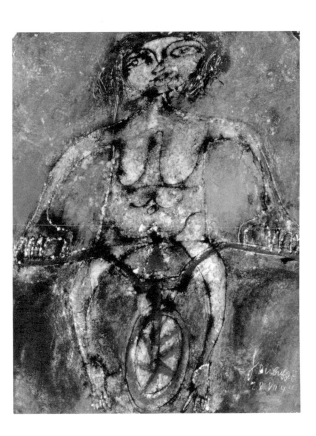

152

La Campagne, juillet 1946
The Country, July 1946

Gouache, 31 x 24 cm.
Gouache, 12½ x 9½"

Collection The Art Institute of
Chicago, Gift of Pierre Matisse

L. Fasc. II, fig. 171.

153

Michaux griffures blanches,
novembre 1946
Michaux, White Scratchings,
November 1946

Dessin à l'encre de Chine sur carte à
gratter, 50 x 31,5 cm.
India ink on scratchboard,
19¾ x 12⅜"

Collection The Art Institute of
Chicago, Bequest of Grant J. Pick

L. Fasc. III, fig. 73.

154

Michaux façon momie, novembre 1946
Michaux, like a Mummy,
November 1946

Dessin au crayon (mine carrée),
31 x 24 cm.
Square lead pencil, 12¼ x 9½"

Private Collection

L. Fasc. III, fig. 75.

155

Limbour cheveux au vent,
novembre 1946
Limbour, Wind-Blown Hair,
November 1946

Dessin au crayon (mine carrée),
48 x 32 cm.
Square lead pencil, 18⅞ x 12⅝"

Private Collection

L. Fasc. III, fig. 78.

*156

Cingria façon caillou, janvier 1947
Cingria, like a Pebble, January 1947

Huile sur papier, 49,5 x 31,5 cm.
Oil on paper, 19½ x 12⅜"

Collection Shelby White

L. Fasc. III, fig. 119.

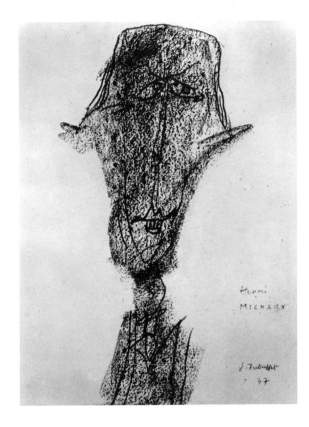

157

Dentiste, janvier 1947
Dentist, January 1947

Encre de Chine, 37 x 32 cm.
Incised India ink, 14½ x 12⅝″

Private Collection, California

L. Fasc. III, fig. 108.

158

Musiciens au désert,
novembre-décembre 1947
Musicians in the Desert,
November-December 1947

Gomme arabique et gouache,
31 x 41 cm.
Paste and gouache, 12¼ x 16⅛″

Collection Musée des Arts Décoratifs,
Paris/Donation Jean Dubuffet

L. Fasc. IV, fig. 30.

159

Chameliers, novembre 1947-avril 1948
Camel Drivers,
November 1947-April 1948

Gouache, 43 x 52 cm.
Gouache, 17 x 20½″

Lent by The Pace Gallery, New York

L. Fasc. IV, fig. 36.

160

Deux arabes gesticulants,
janvier-avril 1948
Two Gesturing Arabs,
January-April 1948

Peinture à la colle, 33 x 40,5 cm.
Distemper, 12⅝ x 15⅞″

Collection Charles Ratton, Paris

L. Fasc. IV, fig. 98.

161

La Fécondation des palmiers,
ca. mars 1948
Fecundation of Palm Trees,
ca. March 1948

Peinture à la colle, 43,5 x 47,5 cm.
Distemper, 17 x 18¾″

Collection Alphonse Chave

L. Fasc. IV, fig. 151.

162

Chameau et empreintes de pas,
janvier 1948
Camel and Footprints, January 1948

Crayons de couleur, 37 x 26 cm.
Colored crayons, 14½ x 10¼"

Collection Fred Mueller

L. Fasc. IV, fig. 200.

163

Arabe à la rose, janvier 1948
Arab with a Rose, January 1948

Crayons de couleur, 34 x 26 cm.
Colored crayons, 13⅜ x 10¼"

Collection Musée des Arts Décoratifs,
Paris/Donation Jean Dubuffet

L. Fasc. IV, fig. 163.

164

Le Désert, janvier 1948
The Desert, January 1948

Crayons de couleur, 32 x 24 cm.
Colored crayons, 12⅝ x 9½″

Collection Lucien Durand, Paris

L. Fasc. IV, fig. 194.

165

Traces de pas sur le sable,
janvier-avril 1948
Footprints on the Sand,
January-April 1948

Dessin à la plume, 19,9 x 15,7 cm.
Pen drawing, 7⅞ x 6¼″

Collection The Museum of Modern
Art, New York, Gift of the artist

L. Fasc. IV, fig. 304.

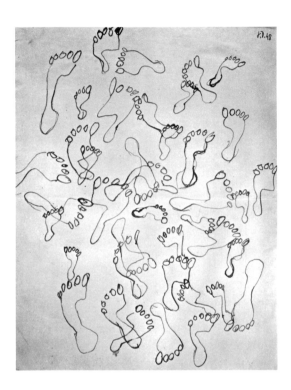

166

Corps de dame, décembre 1950
Corps de Dame, December 1950

Gouache, 48 x 31 cm.
Gouache, 18⅞ x 12¼"

Collection M. et Mme. Daniel
Varenne, Paris

L. Fasc. VI, fig. 128.

167

Corps de dame, juin-décembre 1950
Corps de Dame, June-December 1950

Encre de Chine, 27 x 21 cm.
India ink, 10⅝ x 8¼"

Collection Alfonso A. Ossorio,
East Hampton, New York

L. Fasc. VI, fig. 159.

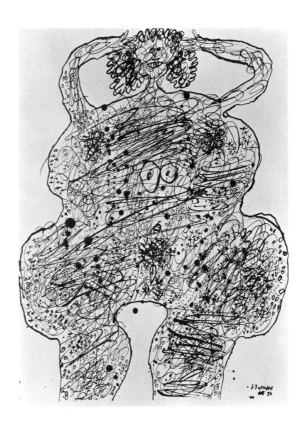

168

Corps de dame, juin-décembre 1950
Corps de Dame, June-December 1950

Dessin à l'encre de Chine (calame et lavis), 33 x 25 cm.
Reed pen and ink wash, 13 x 9⅞″

Collection Mr. and Mrs. Walter Bareiss

L. Fasc. VI, fig. 185.

169

Personnage: femme nue,
ca. février 1951
Figure: Nude, ca. February 1951

Dessin à l'encre de Chine (calame),
31,3 x 23,7 cm.
Reed pen and ink, 12⅜ x 9⅜″

Collection The Museum of Modern Art, New York, Gift of Mr. and Mrs. Lester Francis Avnet

L. Fasc. VI, fig. 186.

170

Personnage dans un paysage désertique, février 1951
Figure in a Desert Landscape, February 1951

Gouache et encre, 25 x 32 cm.
Gouache and ink, 9⅞ x 12⅝"

Collection Hans Pfeiffer, Hannover-Kirchrode

L. Fasc. VII, fig. 26.

171

Table, mars 1951
Table, March 1951

Dessin au crayon, 26 x 21 cm.
Pencil, 10¼ x 8¼"

Collection Alfonso A. Ossorio, East Hampton, New York

L. Fasc. VII, fig. 14.

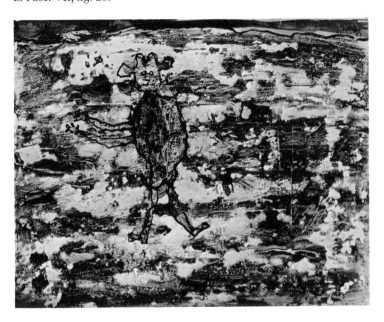

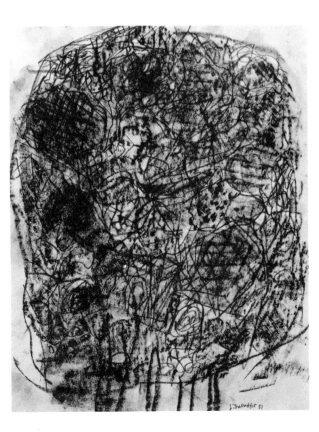

172

Bowery Bum, janvier 1952
Bowery Bum, January 1952

Aquarelle et encre, 47 x 33 cm.
Watercolor and ink, 18½ x 13″

Collection Musée des Arts Décoratifs,
Paris/Donation Jean Dubuffet

L. Fasc. VII, fig. 153.

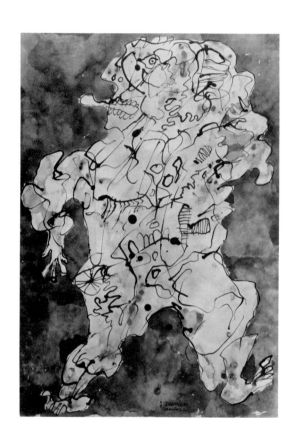

173

*Personnage au chapeau, seins
de côté,* janvier 1952
Hatted Figure, Breasts to One Side,
January 1952

Gouache et encre, 36 x 28 cm.
Gouache and ink, 14¼ x 11″

Private Collection

L. Fasc. VII, fig. 155.

174

*Personnage au chapeau, seins bas
superposés,* janvier 1952
*Hatted Figure, Superimposed Low
Breasts,* January 1952

Gouache et encre de Chine, 36 x 28 cm.
Gouache and India ink, 14¼ x 11″

Private Collection

L. Fasc. VII, fig. 157.

*175

Paysage, juin 1952
Landscape, June 1952

Encre de Chine, 50 x 65 cm.
India ink, 19¾ x 25½″

Collection Dr. Arthur J. Neumann,
New York

L. Fasc. VII, fig. 257.

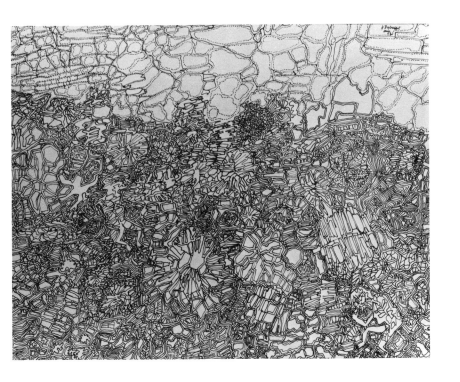

176

Paysage avec deux personnages,
juin 1952
Landscape with Two Figures,
June 1952

Encre de Chine (plume ou calame),
50 x 65 cm.
India ink (pen or reed pen),
19¾ x 25½"

Private Collection

L. Fasc. VII, fig. 262.

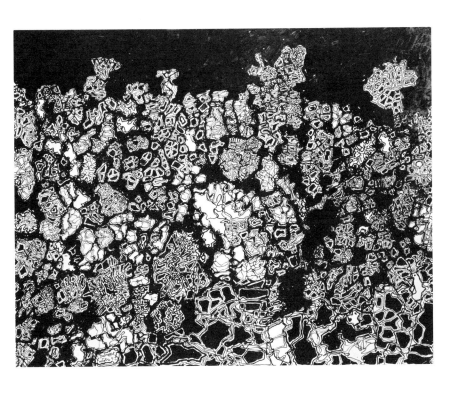

177

Paysage aux filigranes, octobre 1952
Filigree Landscape, October 1952

Encre de Chine (plume et calame),
49 x 65 cm.
India ink (pen and reed pen),
19¾ x 25⅝"

Lent anonymously

L. Fasc. VII, fig. 281.

178

Le Méchu, juillet 1953
Hairylocks, July 1953

Huile sur papier, 65 x 50 cm.
Oil on paper, 25½ x 19¾"

Collection Musée des Arts Décoratifs,
Paris/Donation Jean Dubuffet

L. Fasc. VIII, fig. 83.

*179

Jeux et travaux, 1953
Work and Play, 1953

Lithographie en 5 couleurs, tirée à 65
épreuves, 66 x 50,5 cm.; épreuve hors
commerce
5-color lithograph, edition of 65
prints, 26 x 19⅞"; print "hors
commerce"

Collection Mr. and Mrs.
N. Richard Miller

L. Fasc. IX, fig. 51.

180

Paysage tavelé aux jaillissements,
janvier 1954
Gushing Speckled Landscape,
January 1954

Huile sur papier marouflé sur toile
65 x 50 cm.
Oil on paper mounted on canvas,
25½ x 19¾"

Collection Jean Dubuffet

L. Fasc. IX, fig. 105.

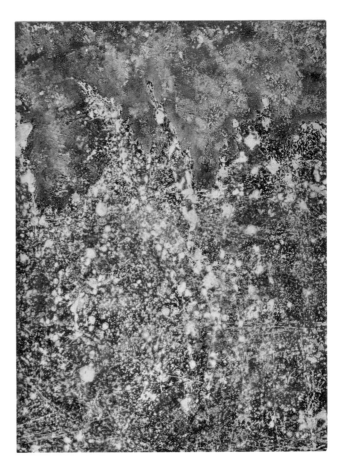

181

L'Homme au pardessus, janvier 1954
Man in an Overcoat, January 1954

Assemblage de morceaux de journaux,
78 x 52 cm.
Newspaper assemblage, 30¾ x 20½″

Private Collection

L. Fasc. IX, fig. 115.

*182

Personnage sur fond rouge,
février 1954
Figure on Red Ground, February 1954

Assemblage de morceaux de journaux,
74 x 41 cm.
Newspaper assemblage, 29⅛ x 16⅛″

Collection Mr. and Mrs. Joseph R.
Shapiro, Oak Park, Illinois

L. Fasc. IX, fig. 145.

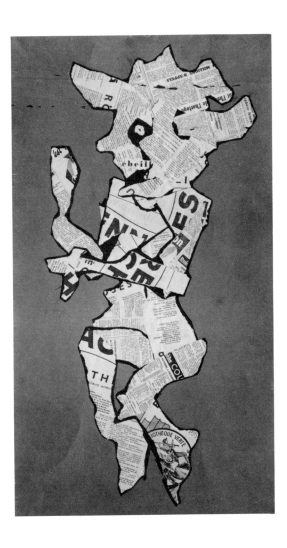

183

Clairière au rôdeur, février 1954
Prowler in a Clearing, February 1954

Assemblage d'empreintes, 60 x 43 cm.
India ink (imprint assemblage),
23⅝ x 17″

Collection Mr. and Mrs. M. Riklis,
New York

L. Fasc. IX, fig. 79.

184

Paysage jaseur, mars-avril 1954
Jabbering Landscape,
March-April 1954

Empreinte et dessin, 63 x 49 cm.
India ink (imprint and drawing),
24⅞ x 19¼″

Collection J. M. de Broglie, Paris

L. Fasc. IX, fig. 89.

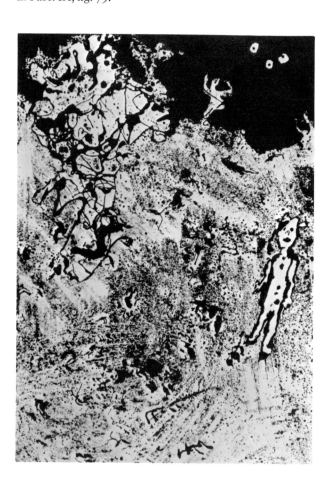

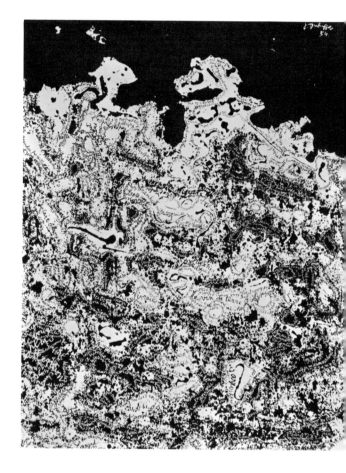

185

Le Pin parasol, ca. avril 1954
The Umbrella Pine, ca. April 1954

Empreinte, 54 x 41 cm.
India ink (imprint), 21¼ x 16⅛″

Collection Musée des Arts Décoratifs,
Paris/Donation Jean Dubuffet

L. Fasc. IX, fig. 92.

186

Eléments dans la nature fugitive, 1954
Elements in Fugitive Nature, 1954

Empreinte, 72,5 x 56,5 cm.
India ink (imprint), 28½ x 22⅛″

Gift of Robert Elkon to the American
Friends of the Israel Museum

L. Fasc. IX, fig. 100.

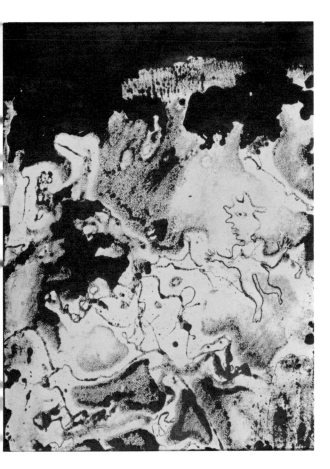

187

Vache lunatique, septembre 1954
Lunatic Cow, September 1954

Aquarelle et encre de Chine,
50 x 38 cm.
Watercolor and India ink, 19¾ x 15″

Collection Stephen Hahn, New York

L. Fasc. X, fig. 120.

188

Vache, 1954
Cow, 1954

Huile sur papier, 38,5 x 50 cm.
Oil on paper, 15⅛ x 19¾″

Collection Mr. and Mrs.
Morton L. Janklow, New York

L. Fasc. X, fig. 131.

189

Vache, décembre 1954
Cow, December 1954

Encre de Chine, 21 x 13 cm.
India ink, 8 x 5¼″

Collection Fred Mueller

L. Fasc. X, fig. 158.

190

Vache, décembre 1954
Cow, December 1954

Encre de Chine, 31 x 24 cm.
India ink, 12¼ x 16⅛″

Collection M. et Mme. Daniel
Varenne, Paris

L. Fasc. X, fig. 159.

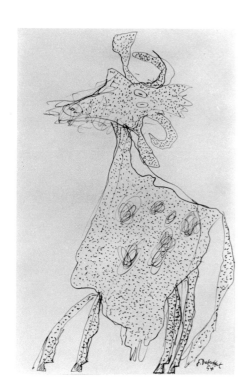

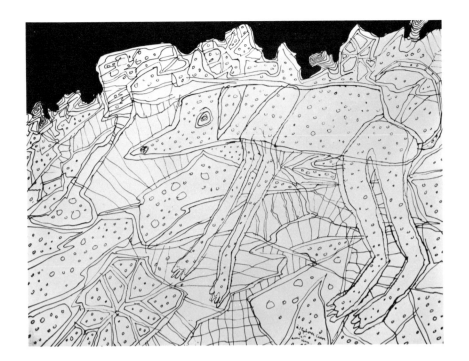

191

Cristallisation du chien,
décembre 1954
Crystallization of a Dog,
December 1954

Encre de Chine, 38 x 50 cm.
India ink, 15 x 19¾"

Collection Alphonse Chave

L. Fasc. X, fig. 209.

192

Inspection du jardin, mai 1955
Garden Inspection, May 1955

Assemblage d'empreintes, 45 x 56 cm.
India ink (imprint assemblage),
17¾ x 22"

Collection Dr. and Mrs.
Irwin R. Berman

L. Fasc. XI, fig. 30.

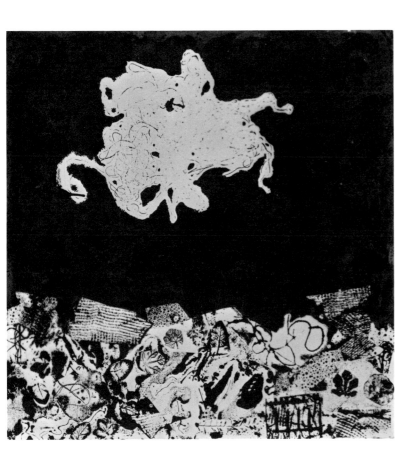

193

Voyage du grand nuage,
juillet-septembre 1955
Voyage of the Great Cloud,
July-September 1955

Assemblage d'empreintes, 68 x 67 cm.
India ink (imprint assemblage),
26¾ x 26⅜″

Collection Mr. and Mrs. I. M. Pei

L. Fasc. XI, fig. 41.

194

Le Chien fouilleur, octobre 1956
Dog Looking Around, October 1956

Assemblage d'empreintes, 51 x 66 cm.
India ink (imprint assemblage),
20⅛ x 26″

Collection Fred Mueller

L. Fasc. XII, fig. 74.

195

Empreinte XIV, janvier 1957
Imprint XIV, January 1957

Encre de Chine, 42,5 x 48 cm.
India ink, 16¾ x 18⅞″

Collection Musée des Arts Décoratifs,
Paris/Donation Jean Dubuffet

L. Fasc. XII, fig. 112.

*196

Marche où tu veux, pas de chemin,
février 1957
Walk where You Wish, No Path,
February 1957

Assemblage d'empreintes,
47,5 x 56 cm.
India ink (imprint assemblage),
18¾ x 22″

Collection Walter Lees, Paris

L. Fasc. XII, fig. 134.

197

Corps d'homme nu, 12 septembre 1957
Nude Man, September 12, 1957

Huile sur papier (assemblage),
116 x 50 cm.
Oil on paper (assemblage)
45¾ x 19¾"

Collection particulière

L. Fasc. XIII, fig. 67.

198

Tête d'homme, étrange fruit,
25 novembre 1957
Head of a Man, Strange Fruit,
November 25, 1957

Huile sur papier (assemblage),
70 x 61 cm.
Oil on paper (assemblage),
27½ x 24″

Collection particulière

L. Fasc. XIII, fig. 124.

*199

Sangre y oro, 13 février 1958
Blood and Gold, February 13, 1958

Assemblage lithographique,
32,5 x 23 cm.
Lithographic assemblage, 12¼ x 9″

Collection Mr. and Mrs.
N. Richard Miller

L. Fasc. XIII, fig. 148

200

Effigie profilée, 23 février 1958
Effigy in Profile, February 23, 1958

Assemblage lithographique,
50,5 x 24,5 cm.
Lithographic assemblage, 19⅞ x 9⅝″

Collection Jean Dubuffet

L. Fasc. XIII, fig. 153.

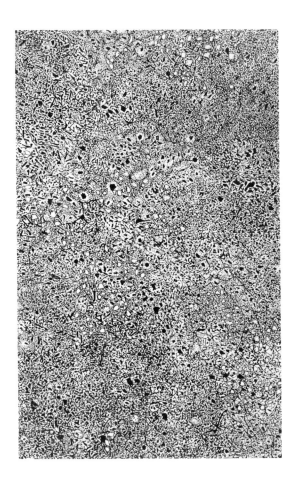

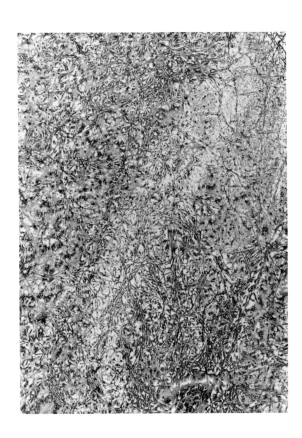

201

Transcription du Sol I,
30 novembre 1958
Transcription of the Earth I,
November 30, 1958

Encre de Chine (plume), 36 x 23 cm.
India ink and pen drawing, 14¼ x 9″

Collection Musée des Arts Décoratifs,
Paris/Donation Jean Dubuffet

L. Fasc. XIV, fig. 114.

202

Résille I, janvier 1959
Meshwork I, January 1959

Empreinte (huile noire), 23,5 x 17 cm.
Oil imprint on paper, 9¼ x 6¾″

Collection Musée des Arts Décoratifs,
Paris/Donation Jean Dubuffet

L. Fasc. XIV, fig. 144.

203

Le Gazon de barbe, mai 1959
Beard: Lawn, May 1959

Encre de Chine (assemblage
d'empreintes), 47 x 28 cm.
India ink (imprint assemblage),
18½ x 11″

Collection Musée des Arts Décoratifs,
Paris/Donation Jean Dubuffet

L. Fasc. XV, fig. 5.

*204

La Source de barbe, juin 1959
Beard: Fount, June 1959

Encre de Chine (assemblage
d'empreintes), 51 x 34 cm.
India ink (imprint assemblage),
20⅛ x 13⅜″

Collection Mrs. Bertram Smith

L. Fasc. XV, fig. 28.

205

Fête de barbe, septembre 1959
Beard: Celebration, September 1959

Gouache (avec papier d'argent),
50 x 34 cm.
Gouache and metal foil, 19¾ x 13⅜″

Collection particulière, Paris

L. Fasc. XV, fig. 70.

206

Fragilité (Série *Banalités*), août 1959
Fragility (*Banalities* Series),
August 1959

Lithographie, empreinte: 45 x 37 cm.,
épreuve d'artiste
Lithograph, imprint: 17⅝ x 14⅝",
artist's proof

Collection The Solomon R. Guggen-
heim Museum, New York,
Gift, Mr. and Mrs. Ralph F. Colin,
New York

L. Fasc. XVI, fig. 328.

207

Symbioses (Série *Spectacles*), août 1959
Symbioses (*Spectacles* Series),
August 1959

Lithographie, empreinte: 44,5 x 38,5
cm., numéro 27 d'un tirage de 30
épreuves
Lithograph, imprint: 17½ x 15⅛″,
number 27 of an edition of 30

Collection The Solomon R. Guggen-
heim Museum, New York,
Gift, Mr. and Mrs. Ralph F. Colin,
New York

L. Fasc. XVI, fig. 342.

208

Paysage avec plusieurs personnages,
mai-juin 1960 (No. 24)
Landscape with Several Figures,
May-June 1960

Encre de Chine, 33 x 25 cm.
India ink, 13 x 9⅞″

Collection M. et Mme. Daniel
Varenne, Paris

L. Fasc. XVIII, fig. 77.

209

Paysage, juin 1960 (No. 29)
Landscape, June 1960

Encre de Chine, 33 x 25 cm.
India ink, 13 x 9⅞″

Collection M. et Mme. Daniel
Varenne, Paris

L. Fasc. XVIII, fig. 82.

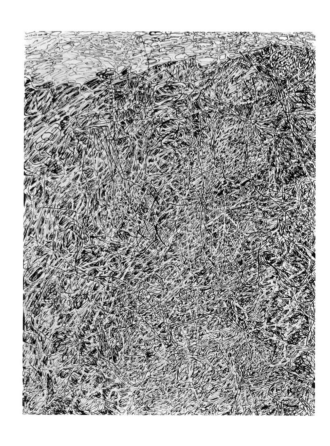

210

Paysage avec personnage couché,
août 1960 (A 91)
Landscape with Reclining Figure,
August 1960

Encre de Chine, 49,5 x 50 cm.
India ink, 19½ x 19¾"

Lent by The Pace Gallery, New York

L. Fasc. XVIII, fig. 186.

211

Aire II, janvier 1961 (B 23)
Area II, January 1961

Encre de Chine, 50 x 67 cm.
India ink, 19¾ x 26⅝"

Collection Musée des Arts Décoratifs,
Paris/Donation Jean Dubuffet

L. Fasc. XVII, fig. 176.

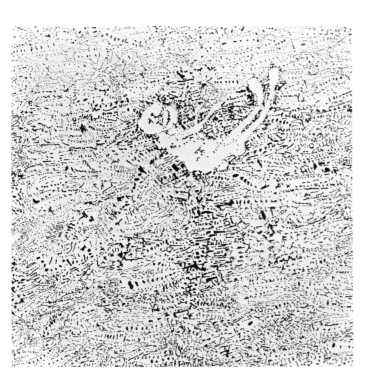

212

Nez carotte, avril 1961
Carrot Nose, April 1961

Maquette pour une lithographie à 4
couleurs, tirée à 55 épreuves,
60 x 38 cm.
Model for 4-color lithograph, edition
of 55 prints, 23⅝ x 15″

Collection Mr. and Mrs. Ralph F.
Colin, New York

L. Fasc. XVI, page 220 (lithograph
illustrated).

213

Personnage au chapeau, avril 1961
Hatted Figure, April 1961

Montage lithographique (décomposition des couleurs), 55 x 38 cm. pour une lithographie à 6 couleurs, tirée à 59 épreuves
Lithographic montage (superimposed progressive prints), 21⅝ x 15″, for 6-color lithograph, edition of 59 prints

Collection Mr. and Mrs. Ralph F. Colin, New York

L. Fasc. XVI, page 221 (lithograph illustrated).

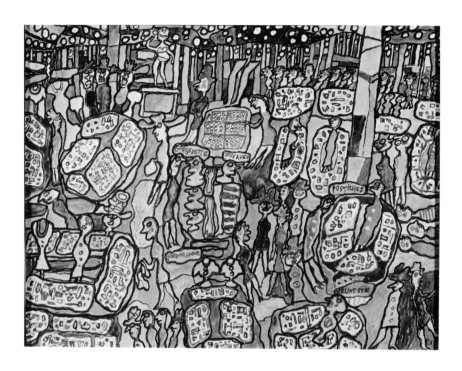

214

Galeries Lafayette, 8 mai 1961
Galeries Lafayette, May 8, 1961

Gouache, 49 x 66 cm.
Gouache, 19¼ x 26″

Collection Musée des Arts Décoratifs,
Paris/Donation Jean Dubuffet

L. Fasc. XIX, fig. 39.

215

Pisseur à droite IV, 27 août 1961 (D 41)
Pissing to the Right IV,
August 27, 1961

Encre de Chine et lavis, 43 x 33,5 cm.
India ink and wash, 16⅞ x 13¼″

Lent by The Pace Gallery, New York

L. Fasc. XIX, fig. 120.

216

Huit personnages, 12 octobre 1961
(DG 17)
Eight Figures, October 12, 1961

Encre de Chine, lavis, gouache blanche,
50 x 67 cm
India ink, wash, white gouache,
19¾ x 26⅜″

Collection Hubert and F. Teri
Damisch, Paris

L. Fasc. XIX, fig. 196

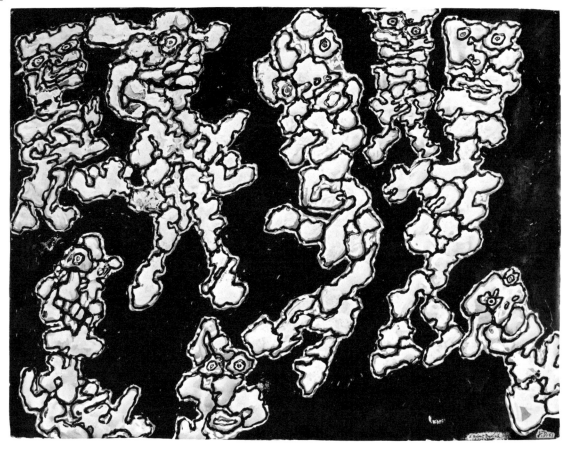

*217

Paysage avec quatre personnages,
6 décembre 1961 (DG 42)
Landscape with Four Figures,
December 6, 1961

Encre de Chine et gouache (collage),
55 x 67 cm.
India ink and gouache (collage),
21⅝ x 26⅜"

Anonymous Loan

L. Fasc. XIX, fig. 233.

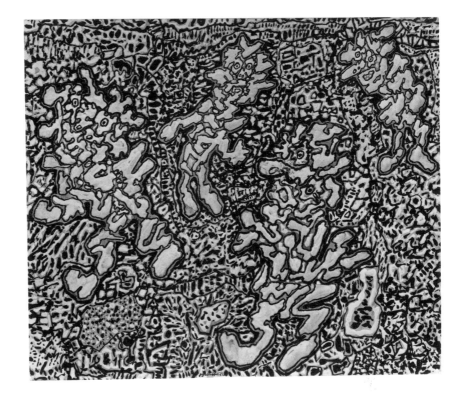

218

Personnage des "légendes,"
1 avril 1962 (DG 136)
Figure from the "Legends" series,
April 1, 1962

Gouache, 67 x 43,5 cm.
Gouache, 26⅜ x 17⅛"

Collection M. et Mme. Daniel
Varenne, Paris

L. Fasc. XIX, fig. 379.

223

Maquette préparatoire de "La Gaya Scienza," 31 juillet 1963 (EG 74)
Preparatory Collage for "La Gaya Scienza," July 31, 1963

Stylobille et gouache assemblage,
27 x 35 cm.
Ball-point pen and gouache
assemblage, 10⅝ x 13¾"

Collection Musée des Arts Décoratifs,
Paris/Donation Jean Dubuffet

L. Fasc. XX, fig. 159.

224

Maison, 12 décembre 1963 (S 34)
House, December 12, 1963

Stylobille sur papier à lettres,
21 x 13,5 cm.
Ball-point pen on letter paper,
8¼ x 5¼"

Collection Jean Dubuffet

L. Fasc. XX, fig. 223.

225

Le Notable, 14 mars 1964 (EG 106)
The Deliberator, March 14, 1964

Vinyle sur papier, 67 x 50 cm.
Vinyl on paper, 26⅜ x 19¾″

Collection Musée des Arts Décoratifs,
Paris/Donation Jean Dubuffet

L. Fasc. XX, fig. 265.

226

Arbre IV, 26 avril 1964 (H 46)
Tree IV, April 26, 1964

Encre de Chine, 33,5 x 25 cm.
India ink, 13¼ x 9⅞″

Collection Jean Dubuffet

L. Fasc. XX, fig. 323.

*227

Samedi tantôt, 14 mai 1964
Saturday Anon, May 14, 1964

Maquette (gouache, collage) pour une lithographie à 8 couleurs, tirée à 142 épreuves, 55 x 40 cm.
Model (gouache, collage) for 8-color lithograph, edition of 142 prints, $21^{5}/_{8}$ x $15^{3}/_{4}''$

Collection Mr. and Mrs. N. Richard Miller

L. Fasc. XX, fig. 325 (lithograph illustrated).

228

Machine à écrire III,
1 juin 1964 (H 57)
Typewriter III, June 1, 1964

Marker et stylobille sur papier à lettres, 21,1 x 27 cm.
Marker and ball-point pen on letter paper, $8^{3}/_{8}$ x $10^{5}/_{8}''$

Collection The Museum of Modern Art, New York, gift of the artist in honor of Mr. and Mrs. Ralph F. Colin

L. Fasc. XX, fig. 340.

229

Tasse de thé, 1965
Cup of Tea, 1965

Mine de plomb, crayon de couleur,
27,5 x 21 cm.
Pencil and colored crayon,
10¾ x 8¼″

Lent by The Pace Gallery, New York

L. Fasc. XXI, fig. 206.

231

Texte putatif (avec deux personnages),
15 mars 1966 (M 48)
Putative Text (with Two Figures),
March 15, 1966

Marker, 27 x 21 cm.
Marker, 10⅝ x 8¼″

Collection Musée des Arts Décoratifs,
Paris/Donation Jean Dubuffet

L. Fasc. XXI, fig. 296.

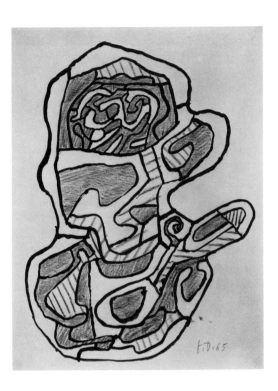

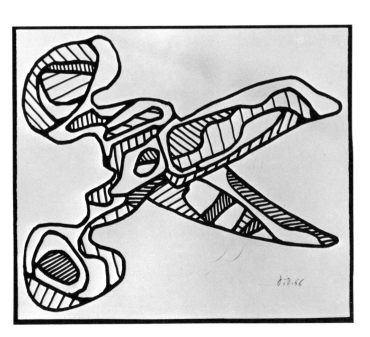

230

Ciseaux, 19 février 1966 (M 18)
Scissors, February 19, 1966

Marker, 23 x 27,5 cm.
Marker, 9 x 10⅞″

Collection Arnold and Milly
Glimcher, New York

L. Fasc. XXI, fig. 246.

232

Banque de l'Hourloupe (dessins originaux pour jeu de cartes)
Bank of the Hourloupe (original drawings for playing cards)

Marker, 25 x 16,5 cm.
Marker, 9⅞ x 6½″

a. *Le Hochet,* 25 mars 1966 (M 63)
   The Baby Rattle, March 25, 1966

   Collection Arnold and Milly Glimcher, New York

   L. Fasc. XXII, fig. 19.

c. *L'Assassin,* 3 mai 1966 (M 103)
   The Assassin, May 3, 1966

   Collection Arnold and Milly Glimcher, New York

   L. Fasc. XXII, fig. 23.

b. *Le Convive,* 2 mai 1966 (M 101)
   The Guest, May 2, 1966

   Collection Fred Mueller

   L. Fasc. XXII, fig. 21.

*d. *L'Ivrogne,* 24 mai 1966 (M 132)
   The Drunkard, May 24, 1966

   Collection Mr. and Mrs. Richard H. Solomon, New York

   L. Fasc. XXII, fig. 52.

e. *La Mouche I*, 31 mai 1966 (M 153)
The Fly I, May 31, 1966

Collection Arnold and Milly
Glimcher, New York

L. Fasc. XXII, fig. 73.

*g. *L' Arbre VII*, 7 juillet 1966 (M 230)
The Tree VII, July 7, 1966

Collection Mr. and Mrs.
Richard H. Solomon, New York

L. Fasc. XXII, fig. 150.

*f. *Le Soldat*, 14 juin 1966 (M 182)
The Soldier, June 14, 1966

Collection Mr. and Mrs.
Richard H. Solomon, New York

L. Fasc. XXII, fig. 102.

h. *La Vache*, 8 juillet 1966 (M 235)
The Cow, July 8, 1966

Collection Arnold and Milly
Glimcher, New York

L. Fasc. XXII, fig. 155.

233

Le Verre d'eau II,
17 novembre 1966 (M 249)
Glass of Water II, November 17, 1966

Marker, 51,5 x 25,5 cm.
Marker, 20¼ x 10″

Collection Max Loreau, Belgium

L. Fasc. XXII, fig. 191.

234

Autoportrait VI,
5 décembre 1966 (M 267)
Self Portrait VI, December 5, 1966

Marker, 26 x 17,5 cm.
Marker, 10¼ x 6⅞″

Collection Max Loreau, Belgium

L. Fasc. XXII, fig. 209.

235

Escalier, 26 avril 1967 (M 434)
Staircase, April 26, 1967

Marker et fond vinyle, 50 x 21,5 cm.
Marker on vinyl ground, 19¾ x 8½"

Lent by The Pace Gallery, New York

L. Fasc. XXII, fig. 402.

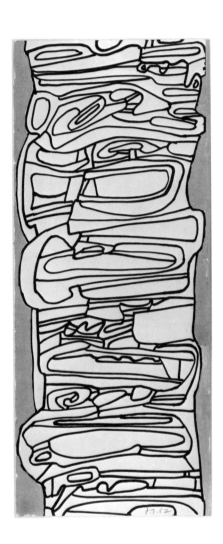

236

Personnage mi-corps, 1967
Torso Figure, 1967

Sérigraphie à 4 couleurs,
moulée sous vide, 54 x 33,5 cm.,
tirage à 50 épreuves, édition 40/50
4-color silk screen, vacuum
formed, 21¼ x 13⅛", edition of 50,
number 40/50

Collection Paul Glimcher, New York

237
Immeuble de douze étages,
août 1970 (P 95)
Building with Twelve Stories,
August 1970

Marker et flashe sur fond Kraft,
60 x 24 cm.
Marker and vinyl paint on Kraft paper,
23⅝ x 9½″

Collection Jean Dubuffet

238

Immeuble de quatre étages,
30 août 1970 (P 92)
Building with Four Stories,
August 30, 1970

Marker et flashe sur fond Kraft,
51 x 31 cm.
Marker and vinyl paint on Kraft
paper, 20 x 12¼″

Collection Jean Dubuffet

239

Danse tricote I, 2 mars 1971 (P 172)
Knit Dance I, March 2, 1971

Marker sur fond Kraft, 38 x 43 cm.
Marker on Kraft paper, 15 x 17″

Collection Jean Dubuffet

240

Monument au coq, 8 avril 1971 (P 188)
Monument with Rooster, April 8, 1971

Marker sur fond Kraft, 42 x 26 cm.
Marker on Kraft paper, 16½ x 10¼″

Collection Jean Dubuffet

241

Echafaudage à la bête perchée,
1971 (P 265)
Scaffolding with Roosting Beast, 1971

Collage au marker sur papier Kraft,
35,5 x 28 cm.
Marker collage on Kraft paper,
14 x 11"

Lent by The Pace Gallery, New York

242

Polymorphie IX, 3 mai 1971 (P 207)
Polymorphism IX, May 3, 1971

Marker sur fond bristol peint,
50 x 65 cm.
Marker on painted bristol board,
19¾ x 25½″

Collection particulière

243

Personnage au chapeau, 1972 (P 283)
Hatted Figure, 1972

Collage au marker sur papier Kraft,
34 x 20 cm.
Marker collage on Kraft paper,
13½ x 8″

Lent by The Pace Gallery, New York

244

Personnage, 1972 (P 307)
Figure, 1972

Collage au marker sur papier Kraft,
34 x 20 cm.
Marker collage on Kraft paper,
13½ x 8″

Lent by The Pace Gallery, New York

245

Personnage, 23 août 1972 (P 352)
Figure, August 23, 1972

Collage au marker sur papier Kraft,
35,5 x 23,5 cm.
Marker collage on Kraft paper,
14 x 9¼″

Lent by The Pace Gallery, New York

246

Bicyclette II, 7 octobre 1972 (P 362)
Bicycle II, October 7, 1972

Marker, 25 x 31 cm.
Marker, 9⅞ x 12¼"

Collection Jean Dubuffet

247

Table, 8 octobre 1972 (P 363)
Table, October 8, 1972

Marker, 21 x 28,5 cm.
Marker, 8¼ x 11¼"

Collection Jean Dubuffet

248

Machine, 8 octobre 1972 (P 364)
Machine, October 8, 1972

Marker, 24 x 28,5 cm.
Marker, 9½ x 11¼″

Collection Jean Dubuffet

249

Arborescence I, 1972
Arborescence I, 1972

Sérigraphie à 2 couleurs, moulée
sous vide, 32,5 x 25,5 cm., tirage
à 75 épreuves
2-color acrylic silk screen on vacuum-
formed plastic, 12¾ x 10″,
edition of 75

Lent by Pace Editions, Inc., New York

Section III Illustrated books

III Livres illustrés

*250

Matière et Mémoire ou les lithographes à l'école, Paris, Fernand Mourlot, 1945
Matter and Memory or Lithographers at School

Texte de Francis Ponge, 34 lithographies de Jean Dubuffet
Edition de 60 exemplaires numérotés, 25 x 32,5 cm.
Text by Francis Ponge, 34 lithographs by Jean Dubuffet
Edition of 60 numbered copies
9⅞ x 12¾"

Collection Mr. and Mrs. N. Richard Miller

L. Fasc. I, figs. 343-376

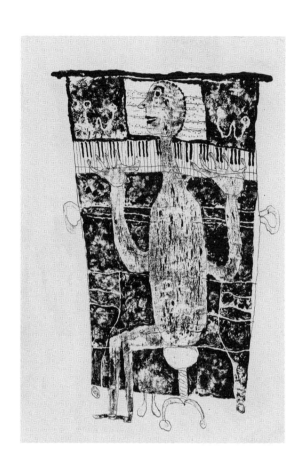

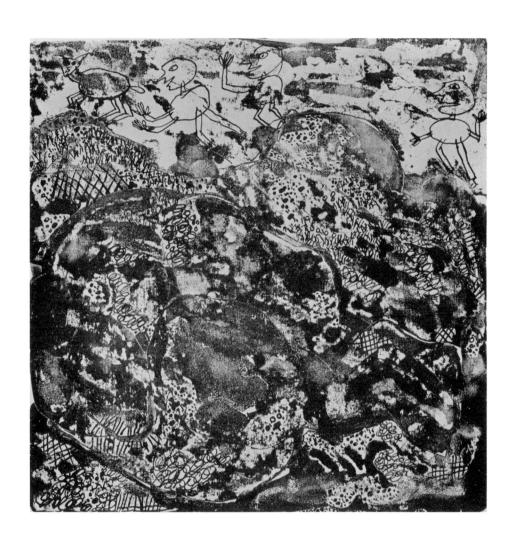

253

Les Murs, Paris, Les Éditions du
Livre, 1950
Walls

12 poèmes de Guillevic, 15 lithographies de Jean Dubuffet
Edition de 172 exemplaires numérotés,
38 x 29 cm.
12 poems by Guillevic, 15 lithographs by Jean Dubuffet
Edition of 172 numbered copies,
15 x 11⅜″

Collection Arnold and Milly
Glimcher, New York

L. Fasc. I, figs. 402-417

254

Labonfam abeber par inbo nom,
Paris, l'auteur, 1950

Texte autographié et illustrations de
Jean Dubuffet
Edition de 50 exemplaires,
23 x 28, 5 cm.
Handwritten text and illustrations by
Jean Dubuffet
Edition of 50 copies, 9⅛ x 11¼″

Collection The Solomon R. Guggenheim Museum, New York; Gift of
Daniel Catton Rich

L. Fasc. V, figs. 179-189.

labonfam abeber
kantele tankoler
itianfil inbou
danltrin safedubiin
esmar estemo rula
bindile sitem pasa
esfe boure dantou
lekouin kesal
putinxe sella

La Lunette farcie, Paris, l'auteur, 1963

Texte de Jean Dubuffet, 11 lithographies originales
Edition de 55 exemplaires numérotés,
43,5 x 38 cm.
Text by Jean Dubuffet, 11 original
lithographs
Edition of 55 numbered copies,
17⅛ x 15″

Collection Dr. and Mrs.
Abraham Melamed

L. Fasc. XVI, pp. 235-238

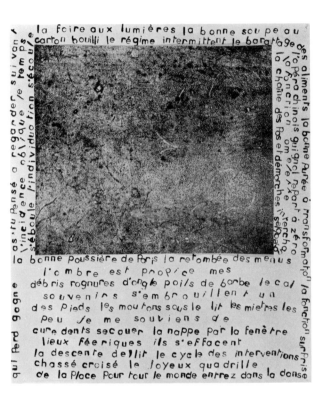

256

L'Hourloupe

Texte et illustrations de Jean Dubuffet (dessins au stylobille rouge et bleu, collés sur fond noir; texte à l'encre blanche), 15-25 juillet 1962
Edition photographique, publié par Noël Arnaud, Paris, pour *Le Petit Jésus,* été 1963, no. 10., 16 x 12,5 cm.
Text and illustrations by Jean Dubuffet (drawings in red and blue ball-point pen, mounted on black ground; text in white ink), July 15-25, 1962

Photographic edition, published by Noël Arnaud, Paris, for *Le Petit Jésus,* summer 1963, no. 10, 6⅝ x 4⅞"

Private Collection

L. Fasc. XX, figs. 1-27

VACHALAÏTE

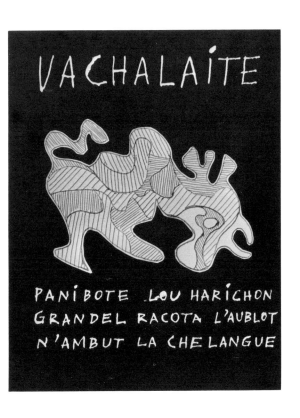

PANIBOTE LOU HARICHON
GRANDEL RACOTA L'AUBLOT
N'AMBUT LA CHELANGUE

NA VOT L'ONFLE ARGACHE
AU MOURNE RADIT L'ORFIAUD
BORLINGUE

RIZÈTE

CANDIPIOTE NOCHETON
LA HAULE CRADASSE LEU
FAITULE NANGIN L'URFLE

257

Le Domino, 24 juillet 1966
Domino, July 24, 1966

Sculpture en polyester, 100 x 50
x 50 cm.
Unique cast polyester resin,
39⅜ x 19¾ x 19¾"

Collection Gerard Louis-Dreyfus

Section IV Three-dimensional works from
the *Hourloupe* cycle

IV Oeuvres à trois dimensions du
cycle de l'Hourloupe

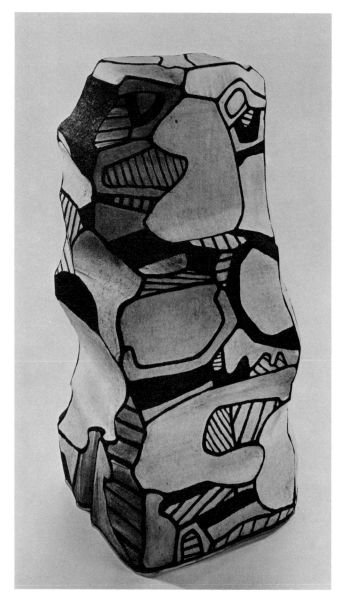

258

Borne au logos VII, 10 octobre 1966
(signé 1967)
Logos Milestone VII, October 10, 1966
(signed 1967)

Sculpture en polyester, 100 x 50
x 50 cm.
Unique cast polyester resin,
39⅜ x 19¾ x 19¾″

Collection Albright-Knox Art Gallery,
Buffalo, New York (Gift of The
Seymour H. Knox Foundation, Inc.)

L. Fasc. XXIII, fig. 23.

*259

Logos II, 17 octobre 1966
Logos II, October 17, 1966

Sculpture en polyester,
121 x 200 x 10 cm.
Unique cast polyester resin,
47⅝ x 78¾ x 4″

Collection Mr. and Mrs. Charles M.
Diker

L. Fasc. XXIII, fig. 27.

*260

Le Verre d'eau II, 3 décembre 1966
(signé 1967)
Glass of Water II, December 3, 1966
(signed 1967)

Sculpture en polyester, 240 x 108
x 10 cm.
Unique cast polyester resin,
94½ x 42½ x 4″

Collection The Hirshhorn Museum
and Sculpture Garden, Smithsonian
Institution, Washington, D.C.

L. Fasc. XXIII, fig. 35.

261

Elément bleu I, 6 juin 1967
Blue Element I, June 6, 1967

Sculpture en polyester, 186 x 98
x 10 cm.
Unique cast polyester resin,
73¼ x 38 ⅝ x 4″

Lent by The Pace Gallery, New York

L. Fasc. XXIII, fig. 45.

*262

Elément bleu II, 10 juin 1967
Blue Element II, June 10, 1967

Sculpture en polyester, 198 x 118
x 10 cm.
Unique cast polyester resin,
78 x 46½ x 4″

Collection Mr. and Mrs.
Robert E. Linton, New York

L. Fasc. XXIII, fig. 46.

263

Elément bleu XIII, 8 juillet 1967
Blue Element XIII, July 8, 1967

Sculpture en polyester, 200 x 98
x 10 cm.
Unique cast polyester resin,
78¾ x 38⅝ x 4″

Collection Mr. and Mrs.
Stephen Shalom, New York

L. Fasc. XXIII, fig. 62.

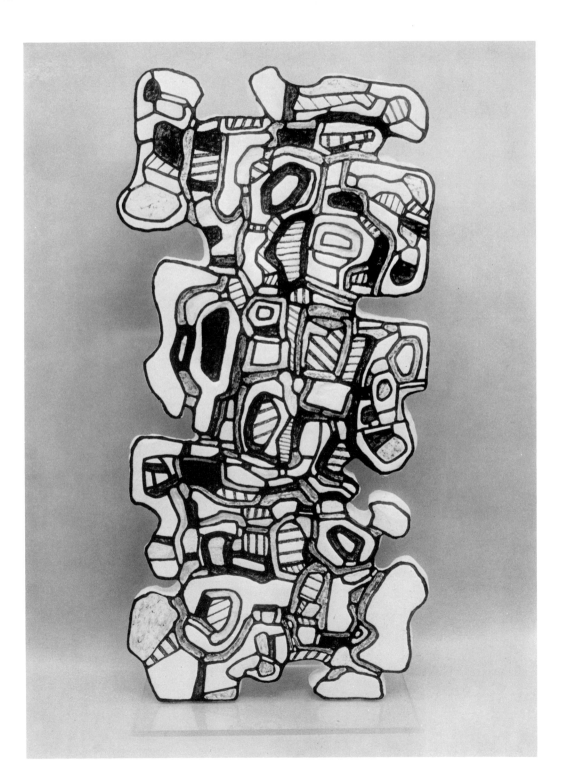

264

Chaise bleue, 18 juin 1967
Blue Chair, June 18, 1967

Sculpture en polyester, 100 x 50
x 50 cm.
Unique cast polyester resin, 38⅜
x 19¾ x 19¾"

Collection Mr. and Mrs. I. M. Pei

L. Fasc. XXIII, fig. 51.

265

Chaise III, 12 août 1967
Chair III, August 12, 1967

Sculpture en polyester, 159 x 73 x
76 cm.
Unique cast polyester resin,
62⅝ x 28¾ x 30″

Lent by The Pace Gallery, New York

L. Fasc. XXIII, fig. 70.

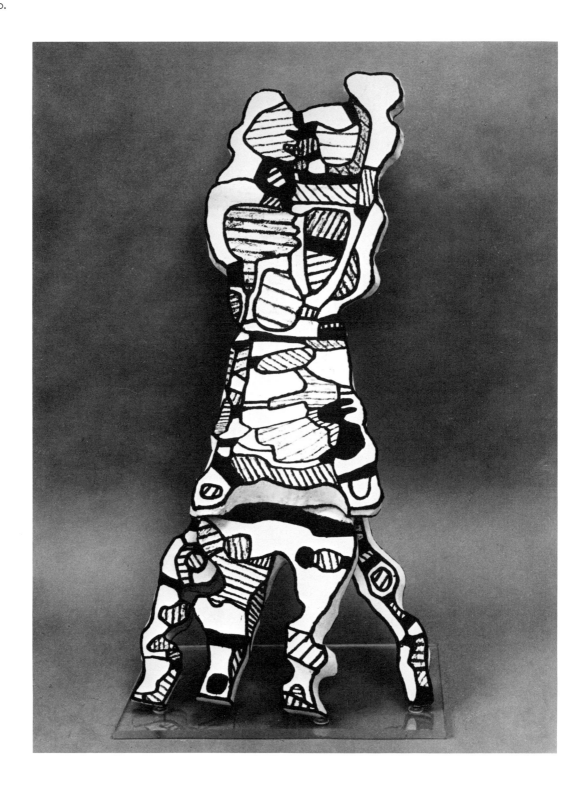

Personnage assis II, 19 août 1967
Seated Figure II, August 19, 1967

Sculpture en polyester, 167,5 x 60
x 65 cm.
Unique cast polyester resin,
66 x 23⅝ x 25½″

Collection Robert and Jane Meyerhoff

L. Fasc. XXIII, fig. 72.

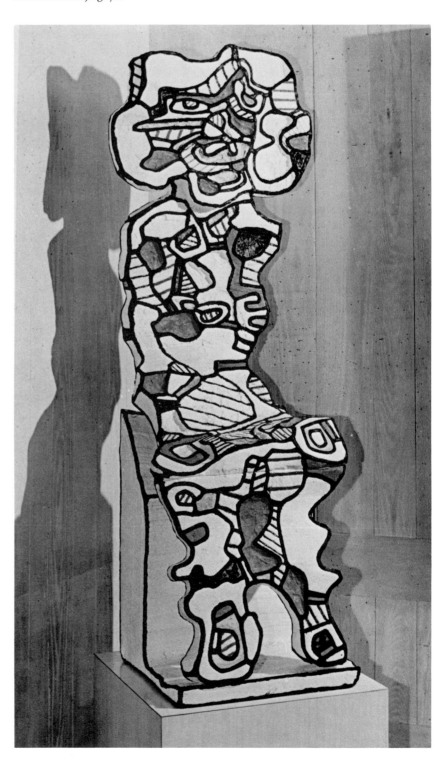

267

Appareil téléphonique, 27 août 1967
Telephone, August 27, 1967

Sculpture en polyester, 85 x 84 x 42 cm.
Unique cast polyester resin,
33½ x 33 x 16½″

Collection Mrs. Eva Glimcher,
Columbus, Ohio

L. Fasc. XXIII, fig. 79.

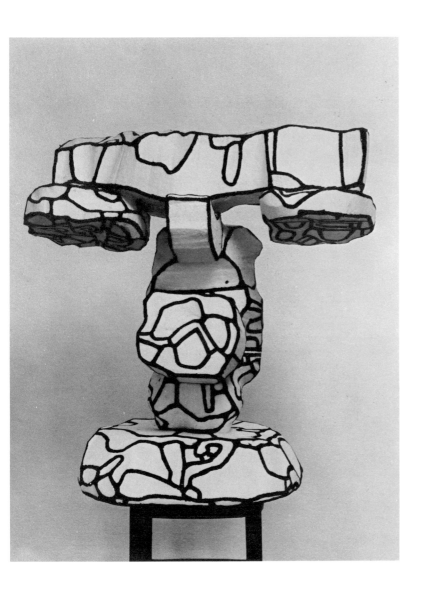

*268

Cuiller à café, 28 août 1967
Teaspoon, August 28, 1967

Sculpture en polyester,
113,5 x 40 x 34,5 cm.
Unique cast polyester resin,
44¾ x 15¾ x 13½″

Collection Mr. and Mrs.
Sidney L. Solomon, New York

L. Fasc. XXIII, fig. 80.

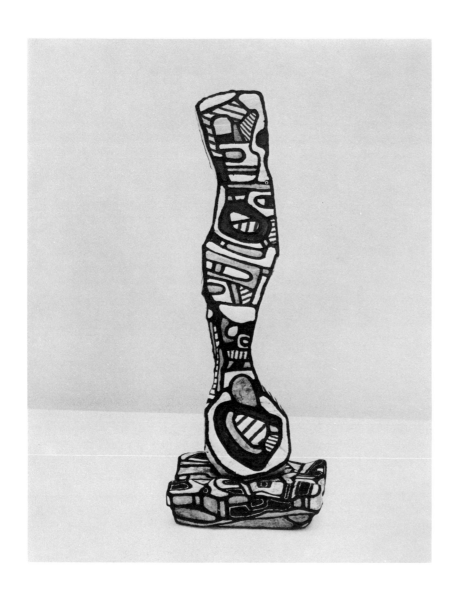

269

Fiston la Filoche, 8 décembre 1967
Fiston la Filoche, December 8, 1967

Sculpture en polyester, 154 x 61
x 37 cm.
Unique cast polyester resin,
60⅝ x 24 x 14½″

Collection Jean Dubuffet

Bidon l'Esbroufe, 11 décembre 1967
Bidon l'Esbroufe, December 11, 1967

Sculpture en polyester, h. 167 cm.
Unique cast polyester resin, 65¾″ h.

Collection The Solomon R. Guggenheim Museum, New York, Gift of the
artist in honor of Mr. and Mrs.
Thomas M. Messer, 1970

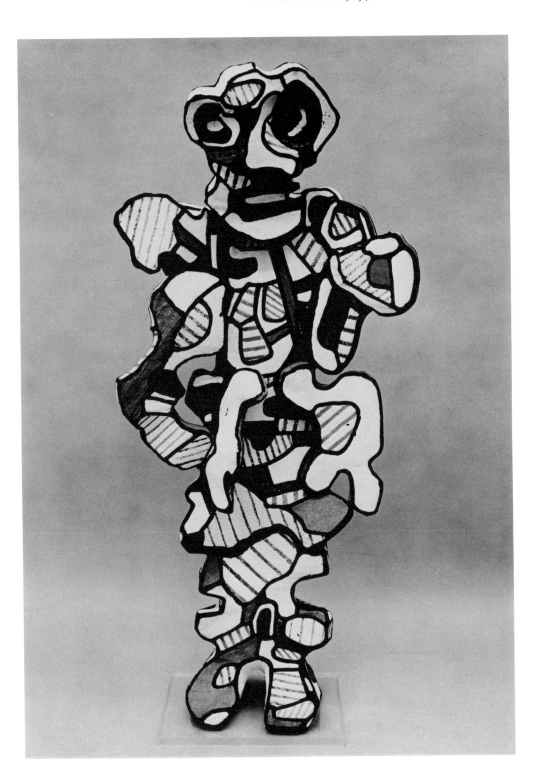

*271

L'Arbre candélabre, 17 février 1968
Candelabra Tree, February 17, 1968

Sculpture en polyester, 220 x 100
x 50 cm.
Unique cast polyester resin,
86⅝ x 39⅜ x 19¾″

Lent by The J. L. Hudson Gallery,
Detroit

*272

Amoncellement au pain, 4 mars 1968
Accumulation with Bread,
March 4, 1968

Epoxy, 97 x 120 x 105 cm.
Epoxy, 38¼ x 47¼ x 41⅜″

Collection Mr. and Mrs.
Gordon Bunshaft, New York

273

Paysage à l'arbre, 12 mars 1968
Landscape with Tree, March 12, 1968

Epoxy, 193 x 140 x 145 cm.
Epoxy, 76 x 55⅛ x 57⅛″

Collection Arnold and Milly
Glimcher, New York

274

Le Jardin d'émail, 15 juin 1968
Enamel Garden, June 15, 1968

Epoxy, 20 x 300 x 200 cm.
Epoxy, 8 x 118 x 78¾″

Lent by The Pace Gallery, New York

275

Paysage au drapeau, 1968
Landscape with Flag, 1968

Epoxy, 99 x 170 x 120 cm.
Epoxy, 39 x 67 x 47¼″

Lent by Galerie Rudolf Zwirner,
Cologne

276

Table à la carafe, 1968
Table with Decanter, 1968

Epoxy, 112 x 139,5 x 115 cm.
Epoxy, 44 x 55 x 45¼"

Collection Mr. and Mrs.
Morton L. Janklow, New York

*277

L'Arbre biplan, 1968
Biplane Tree, 1968

Epoxy, 72 x 61 x 48 cm.
Epoxy, 28¼ x 24 x 19"

Collection Mr. and Mrs.
Peter V. Tishman

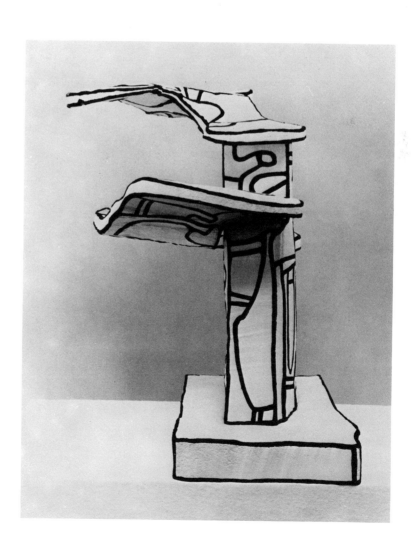

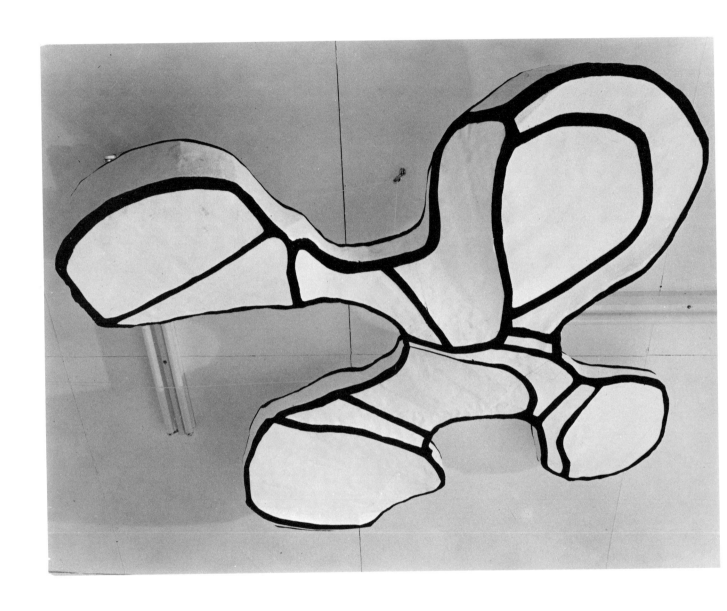

278

Cerf volant le Tétrapode,
18 août 1968-décembre 1969
Kite: Four-Footed,
August 18, 1968-December 1969

Epoxy, 165 x 205 x 44 cm.
Epoxy, 65 x 80¾ x 17¼″

Collection Jean Dubuffet

279

Cerf volant le Nébuleux, 18 août 1968
Kite: Nebulous, August 18, 1968

Epoxy, 150 x 145 x 49 cm.
Epoxy, 59⅛ x 57⅛ x 19¼″

Collection Jean Dubuffet

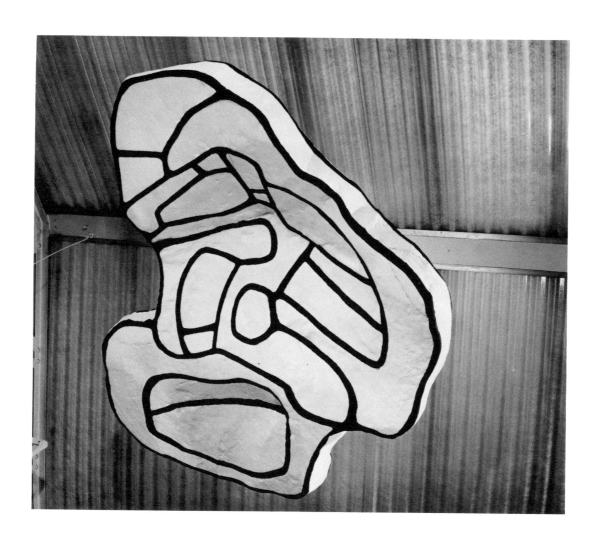

280

Cerf volant la Main céleste,
août 1968-octobre/décembre 1969
Kite: Celestial Hand,
August 1968-October/December 1969

Sculpture en polyester,
230 x 130 x 44 cm.
Unique cast polyester resin,
90½ x 51¼ x 17¼″

Collection Jean Dubuffet

281

Villa Falbala, 28 février 1969
Villa Falbala, February 28, 1969

Sculpture en polyester et peinture
vinylique, 85 x 200 x 150 cm.
Unique cast polyester resin with vinyl
paint, 33½ x 78¾ x 59⅛″

Collection Jean Dubuffet

282

La Tour aux chiffres, juillet 1969
Tower of Ciphers, July 1969

Epoxy, 175 x 85 x 85 cm.
Epoxy, 69 x 33½ x 33½″

Lent by Galerie Beyeler, Basel

283

Table logologique, 1969
Logological Table, 1969

Epoxy, 74 x 117,5 x 70 cm.
Epoxy, 29¼ x 46¼ x 27½″

Lent by The Pace Gallery, New York

*284

Paysage contrapuntique, 1969
Counterpoint Landscape, 1969

Epoxy, 94,5 x 125 x 97 cm.
Epoxy, 37½ x 49¼ x 38¼"

Collection Mr. and Mrs. Charles
M. Diker

285

*Elément d'architecture contor-
sionniste* V, avril 1970
*Element of Contortionistic
Architecture* V, April 1970

Epoxy, 300 x 450 x 180 cm.
Epoxy, 118 x 177 x 70⅞"

Collection Jean Dubuffet

286

Banc salon, avril 1970
Salon Bench, April 1970

Epoxy, 63 x 549 x 405 cm.
Epoxy, 24¾ x 216¼ x 159½″

Collection Jean Dubuffet

287

Chambre au lit sous l'arbre, 4 mai 1970
Interior with Bed and Tree,
May 4, 1970

Epoxy, 97 x 180 x 130 cm.
Epoxy, 38¼ x 70⅞ x 51¼″

Collection Jean Dubuffet

288

La Plante, 1970
Plant, 1970

Epoxy, 72 x 50 x 40 cm.
Epoxy, 28¼ x 19¾ x 15¾″

Collection Dr. and Mrs.
Marvin E. Klein

289

Maquette du "Groupe de quatre arbres", 1971
Model for "Group of Four Trees", 1971

Epoxy, h. 300 cm.
Epoxy, 117¾″ h.

Lent by The Pace Gallery, New York

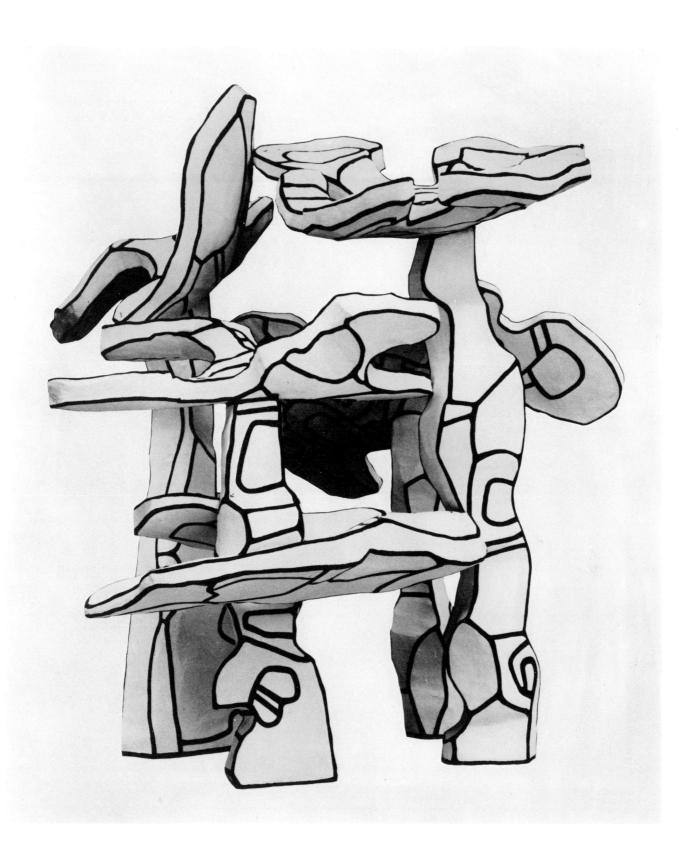

290

Monument au Fantôme, 1969-71
Monument to the Phantom, 1969-1971

Epoxy, 303 x 228 x 174 cm.
Epoxy, 119⅜ x 89¾ x 68½"

Collection Jean Dubuffet

291

Mute permute, octobre 1971
Mute Permute, October 1971

Klégécell entre deux stratifiés polyester,
enduit sternit et peint vinyle,
289 x 385,5 x 4 cm
Vinyl and acrylic paint on klegecell,
glazed with polyester and fiberglass,
113⅝ x 151½ x 1½″

Collection Mr. and Mrs. Morton L.
Janklow, New York

292

Salon au nuage, décembre 1971
Salon with a Cloud, December 1971

Epoxy, 63 x 85 x 220 cm.
Epoxy, 24¾ x 33½ x 86¾″

Collection Jean Dubuffet

293

Plante II: Le Réséda, 25 mai 1972
Plant II: Reseda, May 25, 1972

Epoxy, 167 x 60 x 52 cm.
Epoxy, 65¾ x 23⅝ x 20½″

Collection Jean Dubuffet

294

La Chiffonnière, début janvier 1973
The Rag Picker, early January 1973

Tôle, 251 x 126 x 85 cm.
Sheet metal, 98¾ x 49⅝ x 33½″

Lent by The Pace Gallery, New York

295

Masques
Masks

a. *Masque de théâtre VIII,*
   28 janvier 1972
   Theater Mask VIII,
   January 28, 1972

   Bristol d'epoxy, 58 x 51 cm.
   Epoxy bristol, 22⅞ x 20⅛″

b. *Masque de théâtre XIV,*
ca. 15 mai 1972
Theater Mask XIV,
ca. May 15, 1972

Tôle peinte au polyuréthane,
50 x 42 cm.
Sheet metal with polyurethane
paint, 19¾ x 16½″

c. *Masque de théâtre XVII (Heaume
à la coiffe),* 11 mai 1972
*Theater Mask XVII (Helmet with
Headdress),* May 11, 1972

Polyester peint au polyuréthane,
69 x 68 cm.
Polyester with polyurethane paint,
27⅛ x 26¾″

Lent by The Pace Gallery, New York

296

Coucou Bazar (Le Bal de l'Hourloupe),
1972-73
Coucou Bazaar (The Hourloupe Ball),
1972-73

Tableau animé composé de 47
praticables et 5 personnages en
costume
Kinetic painting composed of 47
décors and 5 costumed figures

Collection Jean Dubuffet

Chronology

1901

Born July 31 in Le Havre. Father a wine merchant.

1908-18

School in Le Havre. Close friendships with Georges Limbour, Raymond Queneau. From 1916 attended art classes.

1918

To Paris to study at Académie Julian which he left after six months to work alone. Met Valadon, Dufy, Max Jacob; friendship with Charles Albert Cingria and later Léger.

1920-22

Studied linguistics, philosophy, literature, music; interest in Dada, psychopathic art.

1923

Trip to Italy. Military service in meteorological service.

1924

Stopped painting entirely until 1933. To Buenos Aires in October for six months, worked as an industrial draftsman in a heating concern.

1925

Returned to Le Havre, entered family wine business.

1930

Founded own wine business in Paris.

1933

Began to paint again part-time, also made marionettes and masks.

1934

Resumed painting full-time.

1937

Abandoned art once again and returned to wine business.

1939-40

Drafted into meteorological service; discharged and returned to Paris.

1942

For the third and final time, decided to devote himself to art.

1944

First one-man exhibition, Galerie René Drouin, Paris. Friendships throughout the 40s with Charles Ratton, Jean Paulhan, Marcel Arland, Henri Michaux, Gaston Chaissac, André Breton and others.

1945

Starts collecting *Art Brut* in France and Switzerland.

1947

First one-man exhibition in New York at Pierre Matisse Gallery. Sold wine business.

March-April, first of three successive visits to Sahara (second, November 1947-April 1948; third, March 1949).

First of a series of *Art Brut* exhibitions held at Galerie René Drouin.

1948

Officially founded *La Compagnie de l'Art Brut*.

Dubuffet installed his collection of *Art Brut* in a location lent to him by Editions Gallimard in Paris.

1949

Publication of Dubuffet's *L'Art Brut préféré aux arts culturels*.

1951-52

November-April; first visit to United States and residence in New York City; delivered *Anticultural Positions* speech at Arts Club of Chicago where his work was being shown. Returned thereafter to Paris.

1954

Retrospective at Cercle Volney, Paris.

1955

Took a house at Vence.

First London exhibition at Institute of Contemporary Arts.

1957

Began to live alternately in Vence and Paris, with stays at Le Touquet.

First museum retrospective at Schloss Morsbroich, Leverkusen.

1958

Special studio for graphic work in Paris; intensive work in lithography.

Retrospective at Arthur Tooth and Sons Gallery, London.

1959

Retrospective at Pierre Matisse Gallery, New York.

1960-61

Major retrospective at Musée des Arts Décoratifs, Paris.

1962

Major retrospective at Museum of Modern Art, New York, shown also at Art Institute of Chicago and Los Angeles County Museum of Art; Dubuffet to New York for opening.

July, beginning of the *Hourloupe* series.

1963

Spent much time arranging and cataloguing *Art Brut* collection.

1964

Important exhibition of *Hourloupe* paintings and drawings at Palazzo Grassi, Venice.

1965

Work on large ceramic panels for University of Nanterre, for which *Nunc Stans* and *Epokhê* are projects; panels never executed.

1966

Retrospectives at Tate Gallery, London; Stedelijk Museum, Amsterdam; Museum of Fine Arts, Dallas (traveled to Walker Art Center, Minneapolis).

Exhibition of *Hourloupe* series at Guggenheim Museum, New York.

Beginning of series of sculptures in styrofoam and epoxy.

1967

Donation of portion of collection of his own work to Musée des Arts Décoratifs, Paris.

Publication of collection of Dubuffet's writings: *Prospectus et tous écrits suivants,* Gallimard, Paris, 2 volumes, edited, and with an introduction by Hubert Damisch.

Started work on architectural structures and *Le Cabinet Logologique,* environment in form of a room.

April-June, first museum exhibition of *Art Brut* at Musée des Arts Décoratifs, Paris.

1968

First *amoncellements* in styrofoam and epoxy.

Exhibitions of *Tour aux Figures,* Museum of Modern Art, New York, *Architectures,* Musée des Arts Décoratifs, Paris.

1969

Numerous commissions for outdoor monumental sculpture.

February, begins work on *Villa Falbala,* executes first styrofoam model for it.

Execution (through 1970) of garden in the form of a cave, *Jardin d'hiver* (dated 1968).

Retrospective at Museum of Fine Arts, Montreal.

1970

Installs studio for monumental works at Périgny; breaks ground there for *Villa Falbala.*

Le Cabinet Logologique shown at Centre National d'Art Contemporain, Paris.

Exhibition of monuments and architecture at Art Institute of Chicago.

1971

Beginning of series of *praticables* for theater and series of *costumes de théâtre.*

1972

August, Dubuffet's collection of *Art Brut* officially given to the city of Lausanne.

Completion of monumental commission, *Group of Four Trees* at Chase Manhattan Plaza, New York; inauguration October 24, 1972.

Catalogue des travaux de Jean Dubuffet, Paris, Jean-Jacques Pauvert, éditeur; Weber éditeur

The following is a listing of the volumes (fascicules) of the *catalogue raisonné* of Jean Dubuffet's work. Organized chronologically, each fascicule includes an introduction by Max Loreau, a complete and fully illustrated inventory of the works of each period, press excerpts, selected bibliography and index. A summary of each period is provided below in order to orient the visitor to the present exhibition.

I. *Marionnettes de la ville et de la campagne* (1942-1945) (Marionettes of the city and the country)

City and country scenes in which the style is reminiscent of *Art Brut:* schematic figures, vibrant color distributed in flat planes, no perspective. In 1944, the colors become more somber and monochrome, inspired by interest in graffiti.

II. *Mirobolus, Macadam et Cie* (1945-1946) (Mirobolus, Macadam and Co.)

Experiments with diverse "non-art" materials (thick impasto incorporating sand, pebbles, glass). Large single figures in a frontal hieratic stance are incised or built up in these materials. Low-key, sometimes iridescent colors.

III. *Plus beaux qu'ils croient (Portraits)* (1946-1947) [Handsomer than they think (Portraits)]

Imaginary portraits of writers and artists among Dubuffet's friends in which the general characteristics of each — as Dubuffet subjectively sees them or freely extrapolates — are captured. No attempt at literal resemblance.

IV. *Roses d' Allah, clowns du désert* (1947-1949) (Roses of Allah, clowns of the desert)

Three visits to North Africa inspire images of desert life: the vast uninterrupted landscapes, the insignificance and anonymity of man, the "guttural" quality of Arab life and language. Small formats, many works on paper, experiments with materials (colored crayons, distemper).

V. *Paysages grotesques* (1949-1950) (Grotesque landscapes)

Landscapes animated with figures, and unified by a general chromatic tone, probably inspired by the artist's desert experience. The transparent line figures wander at random or are still, incised into the slight gradations of several layers of color on the field.

VI. *Corps de dames* (1950-1951) (Nude female figures)

"Celebrations" of the female who appears as a cult object, a flattened effigy, an eroticized landscape. Simultaneously an assault on the classic ideal of the female nude. Experiments with oil emulsions produce the dissolved contours, bleeding colors and fluid textures of some of these paintings.

VII. *Tables paysagées, paysages du mental, pierres philosophiques* (1950-1952)
(Landscaped tables, tables of the mind, stones of philosophy)

Heavy relief, sometimes high varnish, producing a contradiction between the abstract (mental) imagery and a strong physical presence. Deliberate submission to the accidents of materials (plastic resins). 1951-52: series of ink drawings: *Terres radieuses* (Radiant Lands), in which an uninterrupted cellular structure forecasts the *Hourloupe* cycle.

VIII. *Lieux momentanés, pâtes battues* (1952-1953)
(Momentary places, mixed impasto)

Vast landscapes in which the artist's incisive gesture and high color animate the surface rather than configurations induced by the materials themselves.

IX. *Assemblages d'empreintes* (1953-1954)
(Imprint assemblages)

The first butterfly-wing assemblages of 1953 show interest in cellular form; they also determine the color and structure of the imagery. In the assemblage of fragments of ink transfer drawings into ephemeral landscapes with fantastic figures, once again the materials guide the artist's inspiration and hand.

X. *Vaches, Petites statues de la vie précaire* (1954)
(Cows, little statues of precarious existence)

Small figurines in clinker, sponge, charcoal, whose very existence is threatened by the fragility and imminent decay of their substance. Pastoral scenes in which the protagonists are anti-heroic (tragic) cows.

XI. *Charrettes, jardins, personnages monolithes* (1955-1956)
(Carts, gardens, monolithic figures)

Painted in Vence in the south of France. Speckled landscapes, burned-out color, brittle contours, depiction of dry vegetation, pebbly soil. Second series of butterfly-wing assemblages depicting gardens in which the artist reinforces the web-like structures through paint.

XII. *Tableaux d' assemblages* (1955-1957)
(Assemblages of painted canvas)

After the India ink assemblages, the artist executed assemblages of fragments of spattered canvas, encouraging unexpected juxtapositions and accidental configurations. The mosaic pattern of irrational forms anticipates the *Hourloupe*.

XIII. *Célébration du sol I, lieux cursifs, texturologies, topographies* (1957-1958)
(Celebration of the earth I, cursive places, texturologies, topographies)

Interest in texture leads to the representation of vast "topographies" or undetermined landscapes. The assemblage technique is used in some of them, soon to be replaced by all-over painterly grounds.

XIV. *Célébration du sol II, texturologies, topographies* (1958-1959)
(Celebration of the earth II, texturologies, topographies)

Further development of the preceding period. All indications of scale are abolished, creating an ambiguity between a literal fragment of the earth and a vast undifferentiated landscape.

XV. *As-tu cueilli la fleur de barbe?* (1959)
(Did you pick the beard's flower?)

Series of beard-scapes, beard effigies, beards in every form. Accent on texture through graphic incident. Celebration of the beard as hair, but also evoking grass, dust, natural accidents and particles of the soil.

XVI. *Les Phénomènes* (1958-1963)
(Phenomena)

Lithographic encyclopedia of textures relating to diverse natural phenomena. 15 volumes of black and white lithographs, 9 volumes of color lithographs.

XVII. *Matériologies* (1958-1960)
(Materiologies)

Assemblages of botanical materials: all kinds of leaves and vegetation, dried banana peels, bark. Desire to bow to nature. October 1959: second series of small figurines made of driftwood, papier mâché, metal foil.

XVIII. *Dessins* (1960-1961)
(Drawings)

Three series of ink drawings in which effects of texture and problems of figure-ground contiguity are explored.

XIX. *Paris Circus* (1961-1962)
      (Paris Circus)

First long stay in Paris since 1954. Retreat from fascination
with natural materials; return to the stage of marionettes
(1943-44): street scenes, shops, restaurants; bright lush
colors; works more densely (and ambiguously) orchestrated
than the works of 1943-44. Birth of the *Legends* series of
phantasmagoric polychrome apparitions which prefigure
the *Hourloupe*.

XX. *Hourloupe I* (1962-1964)

July 1962: red and blue ball-point doodlings give rise to
aberrational configurations, purely imaginary cellular figures.
Progressive restriction of the palette in gouaches and paint-
ings; progressive dematerialization and abstraction of images.
Interest in "errors" and irrational wanderings of the mind.
December 1963: begins to work with vinyl paint.

XXI. *Hourloupe II* (1964-1966)

Emphasis on vast mental landscapes consisting of larger
modules (cf. *Nunc Stans*) and in which the imagery is less
easily decipherable. Series of isolated domestic objects *as*
landscapes. Finally the painting becomes a pure irrational
chain of non-signifying forms.

XXII. *Cartes, ustensiles* (1964-1967)
       (Playing cards, utensils)

1964: Creation of *Hourloupe* playing cards *(Banque de
l'Hourloupe, Algèbre de l'Hourloupe)* so that each may try
his hand at the game of chance. "Utopic" (or non-functional)
"utensils", utopic places, each of which contains a world.

XXIII. *Sculptures Peintes* (1966-1967)
       (Painted sculptures)

The equivocal universe of the *Hourloupe* translated into three
dimensions: road markers, human figures, accumulations of
domestic objects, chairs, all of which are non-functional,
ambiguous.

XXIV. *Edifices, Monuments*   (in preparation)
       (Edifices, monuments)

Utopic architectures, environments, town houses, rooms,
monuments.

Photographic Credits

EXHIBITION 73/3

8,000 copies of this catalogue designed by Malcolm Grear,

typeset by Craftsman Type Inc.

have been printed by The Meriden Gravure Company

in April 1973 for the Trustees of

The Solomon R. Guggenheim Foundation